George Clooney Coloring Book

Hollywood Charmer and Gentleman, Multiple Academy Award Winner and Hot Actor Inspired Adult Coloring Book

Becca Baldwin

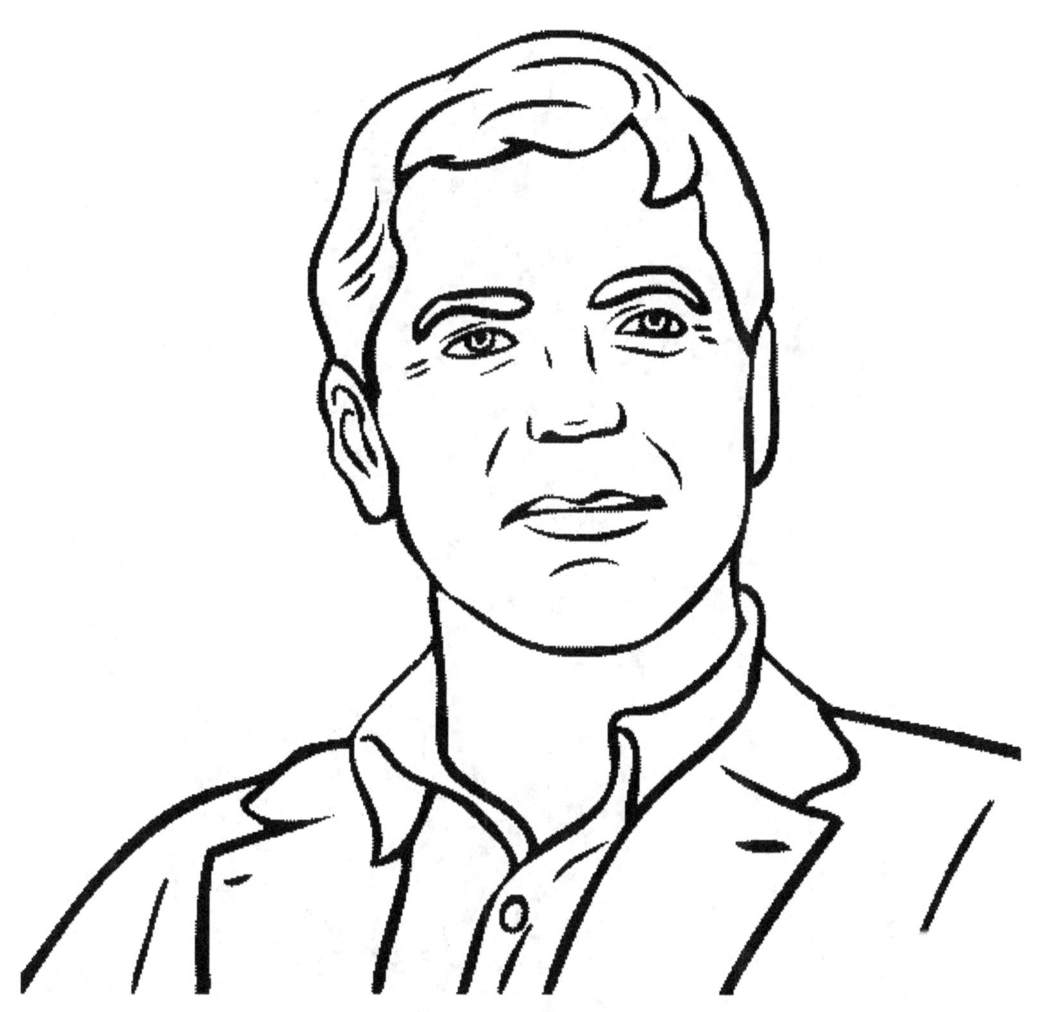

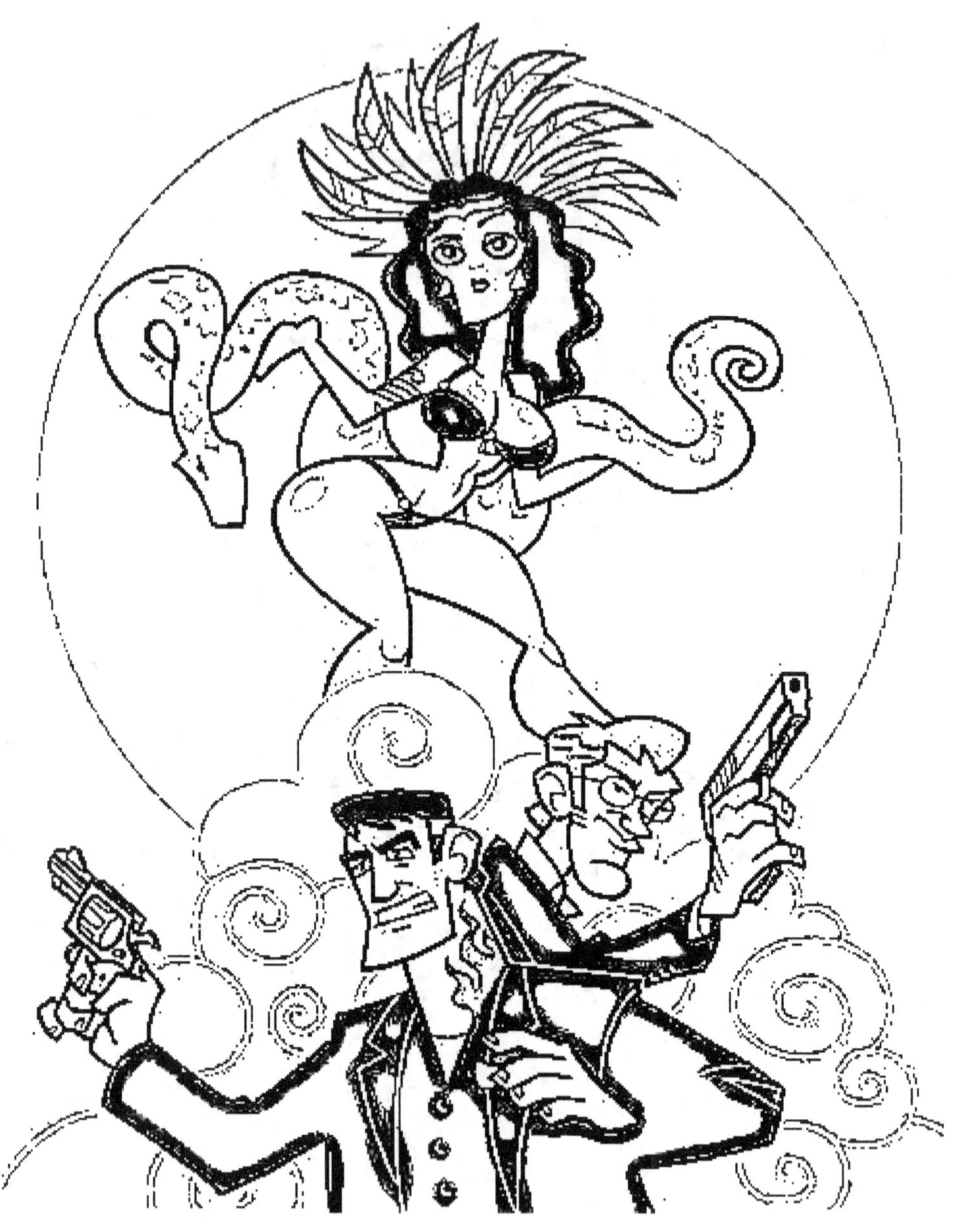

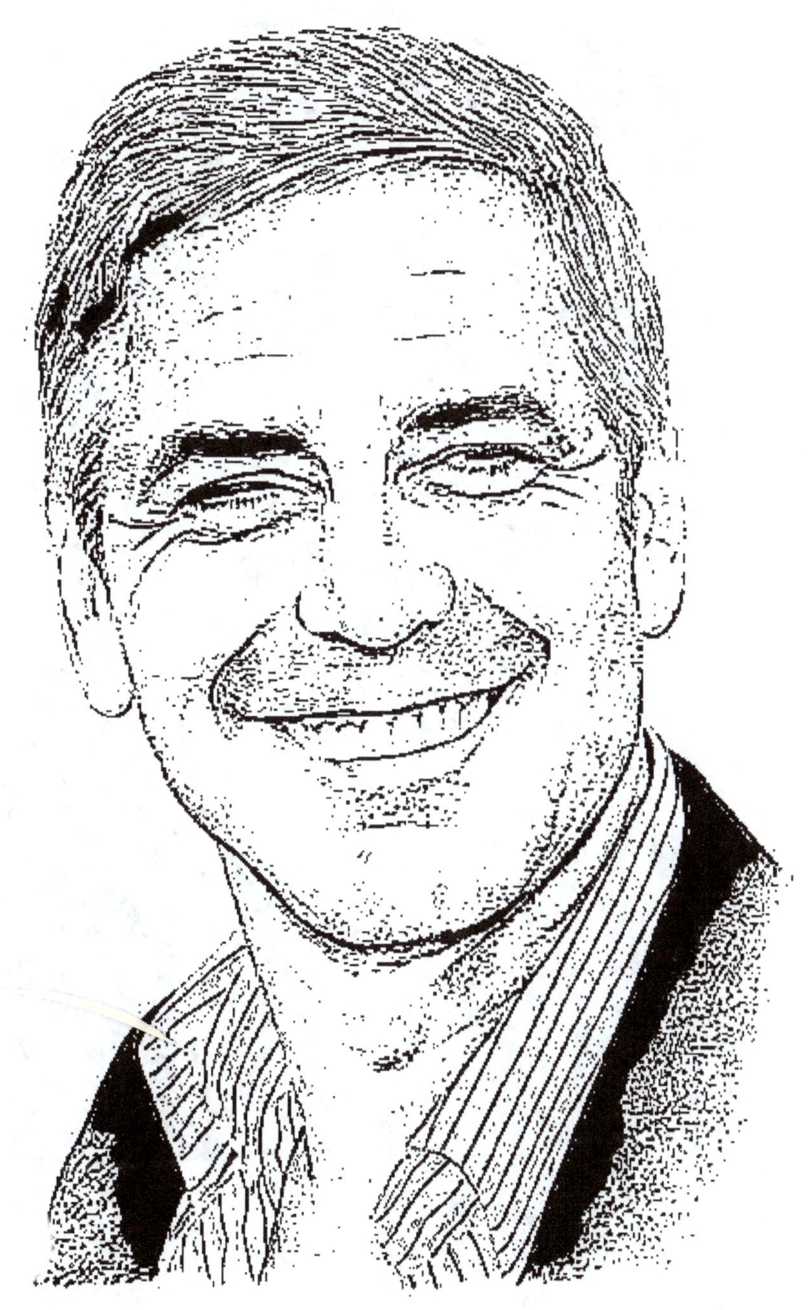

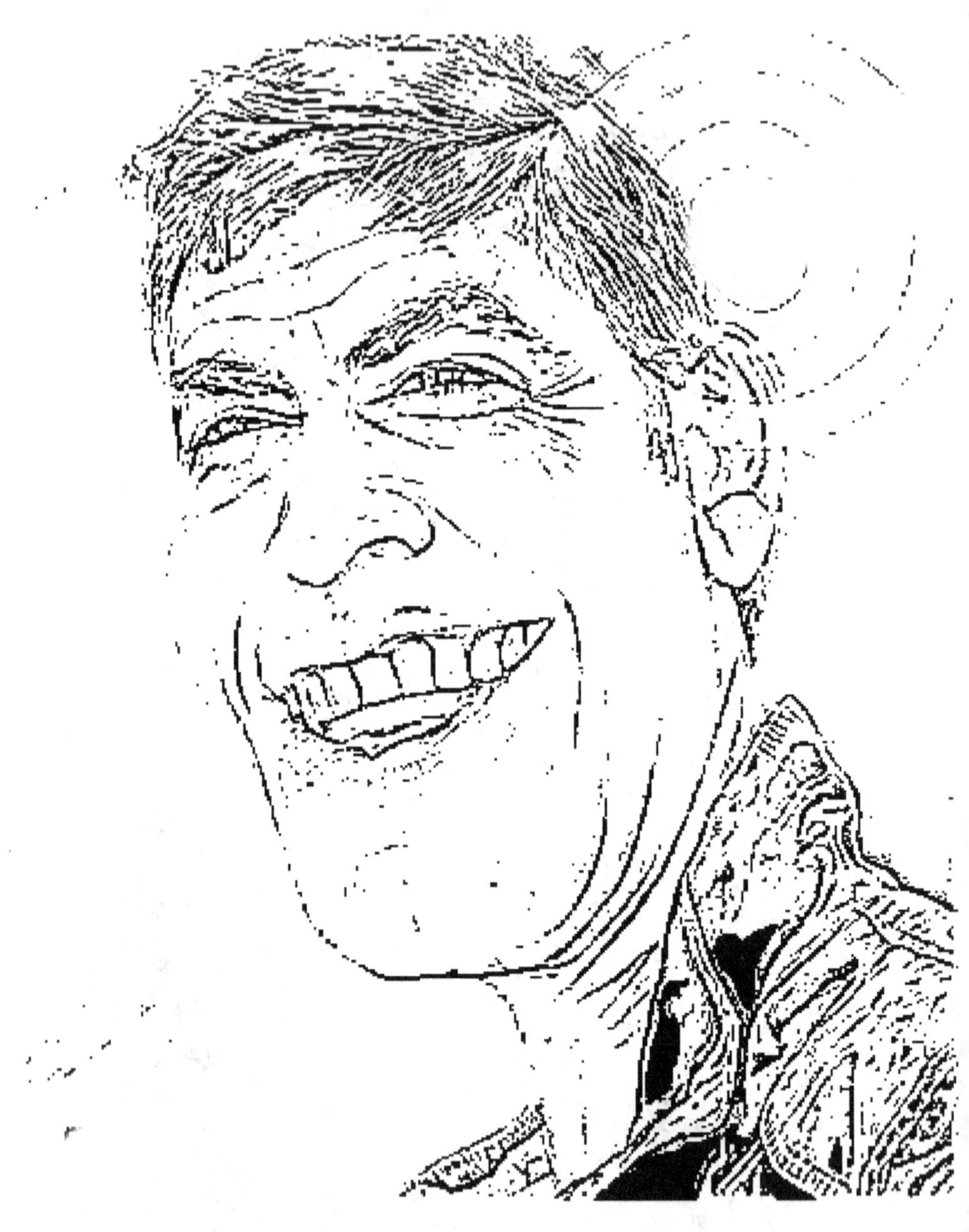

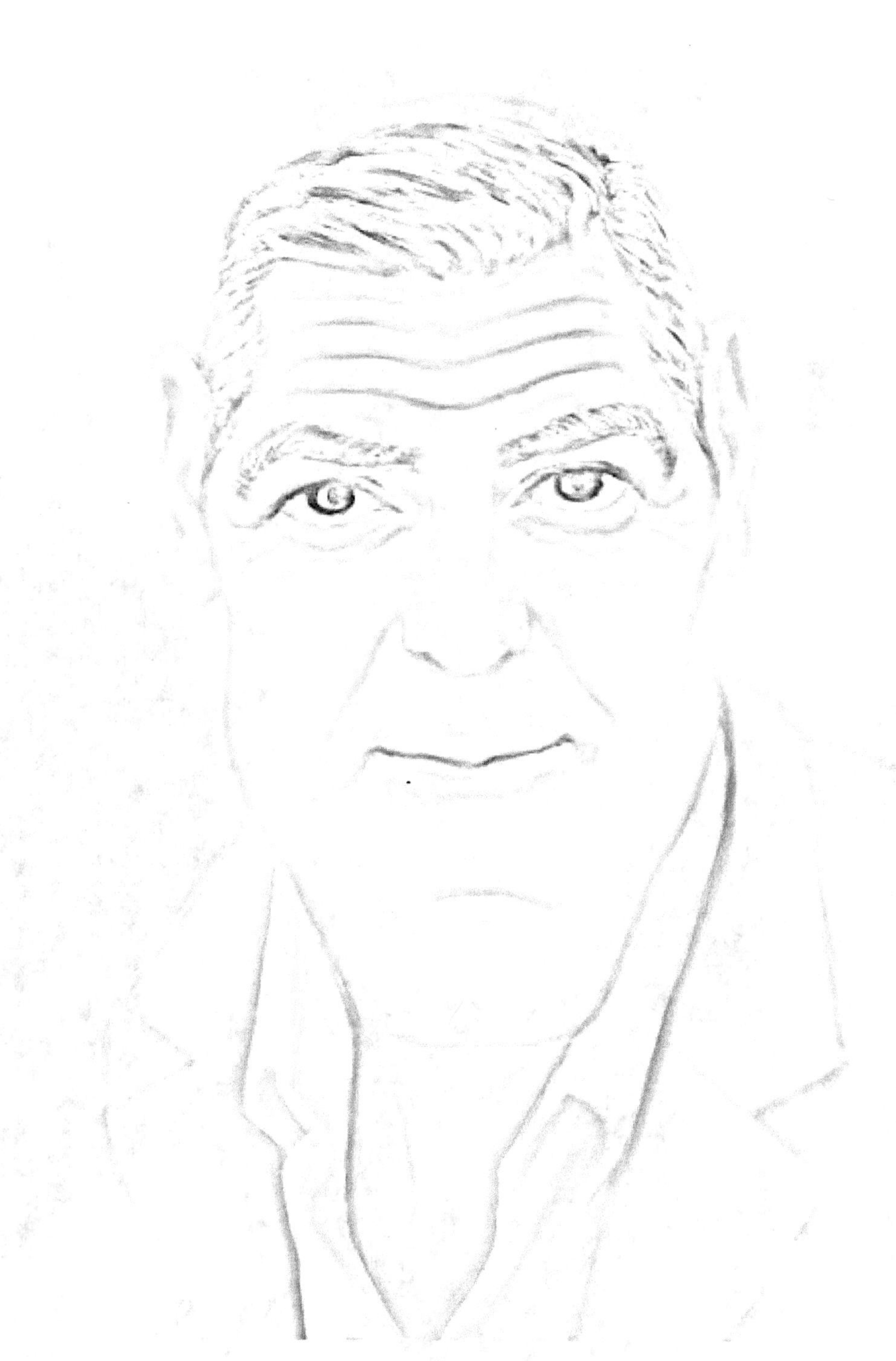

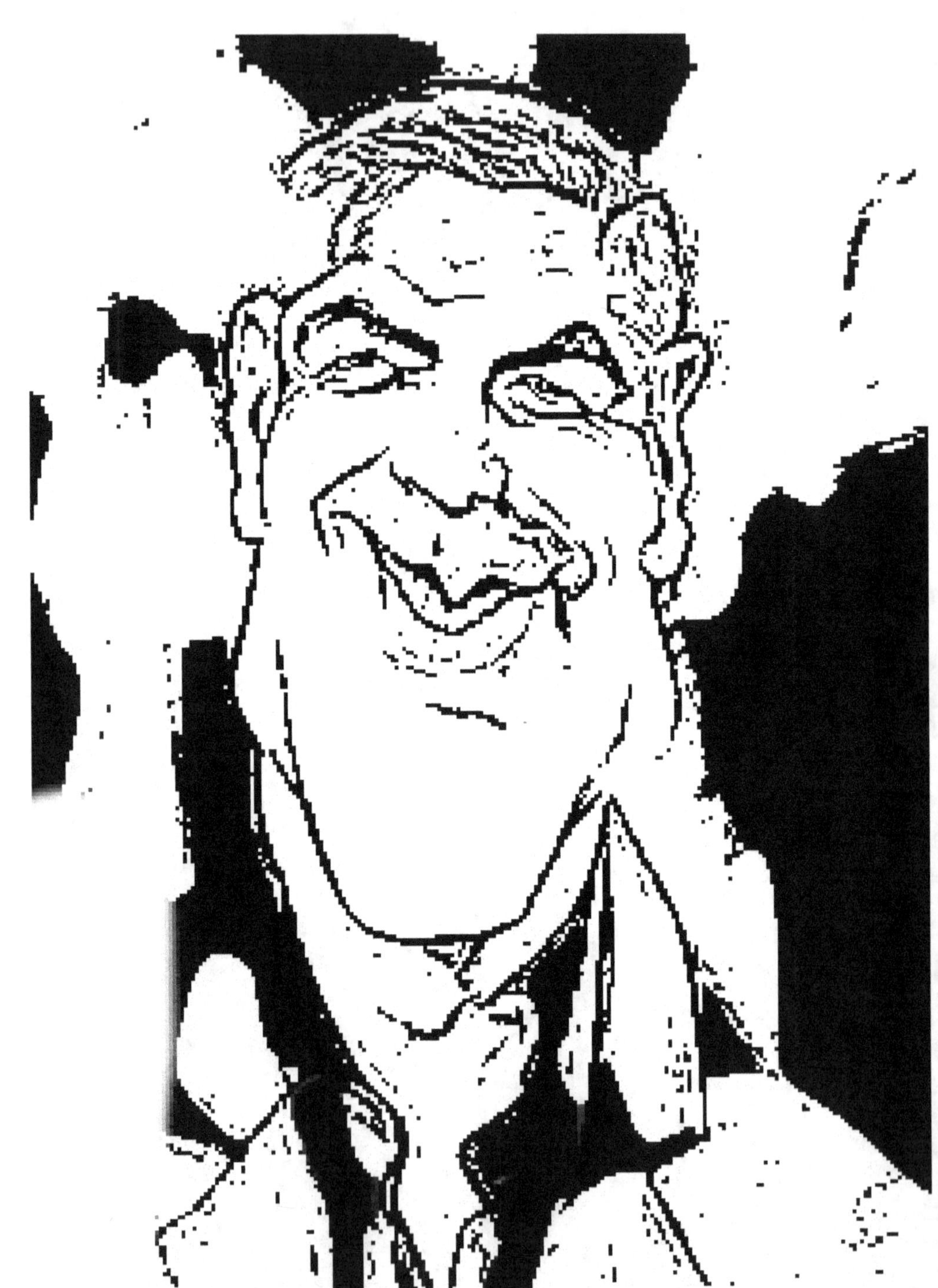

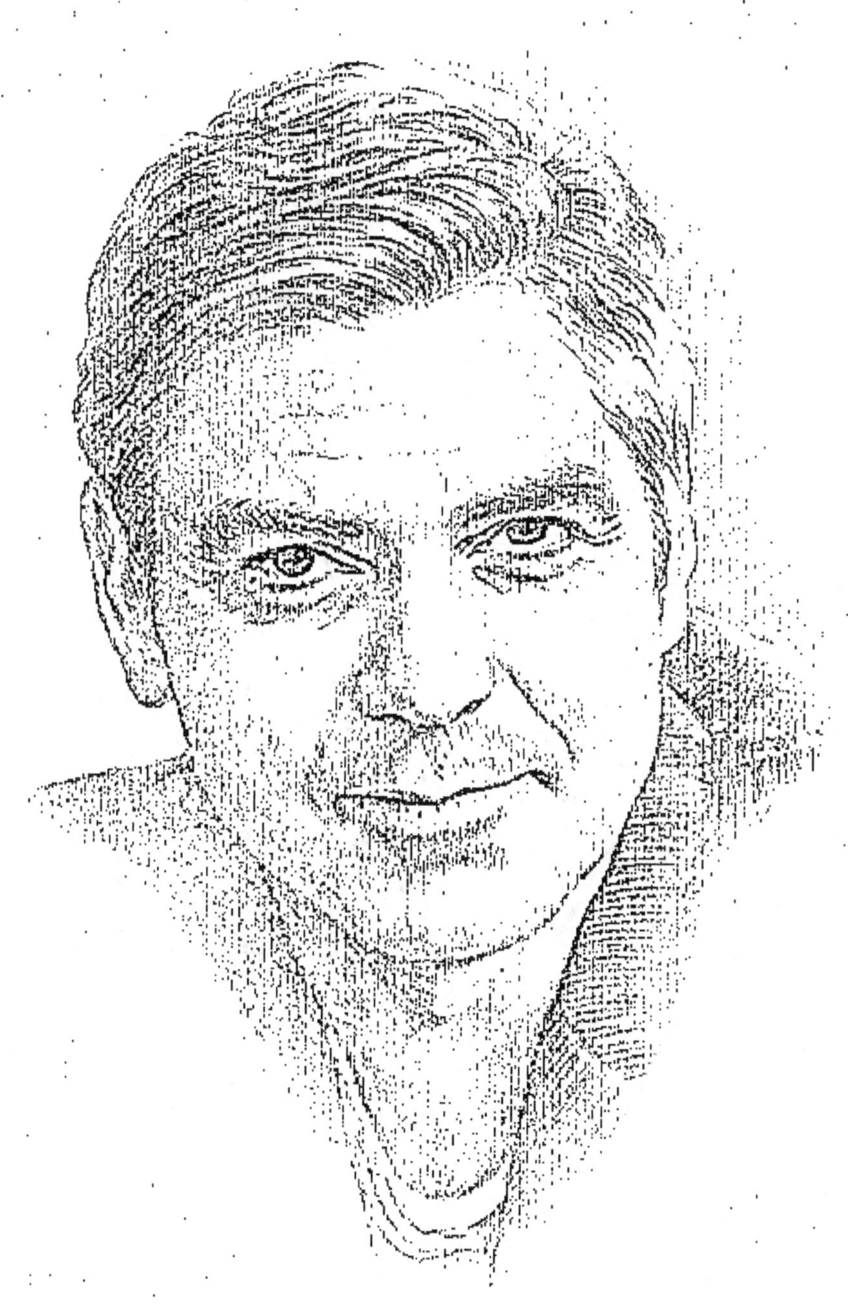

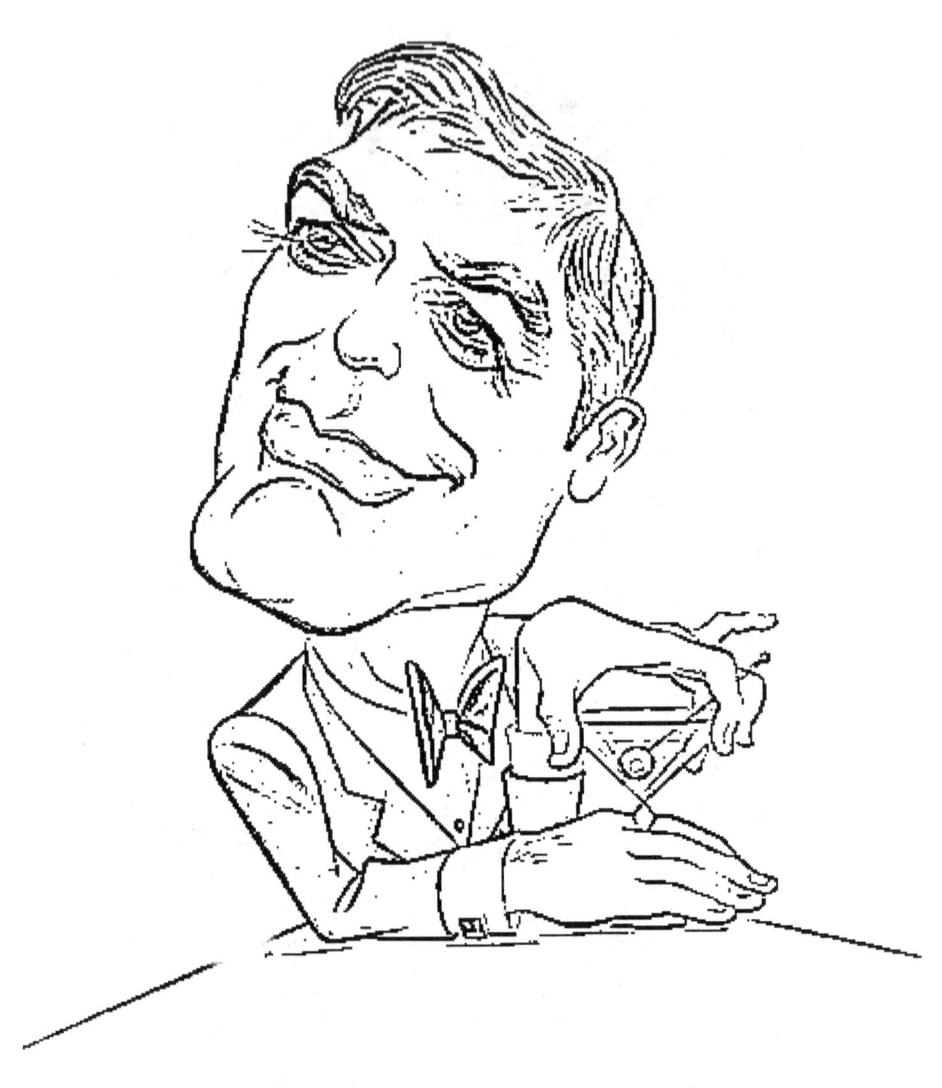

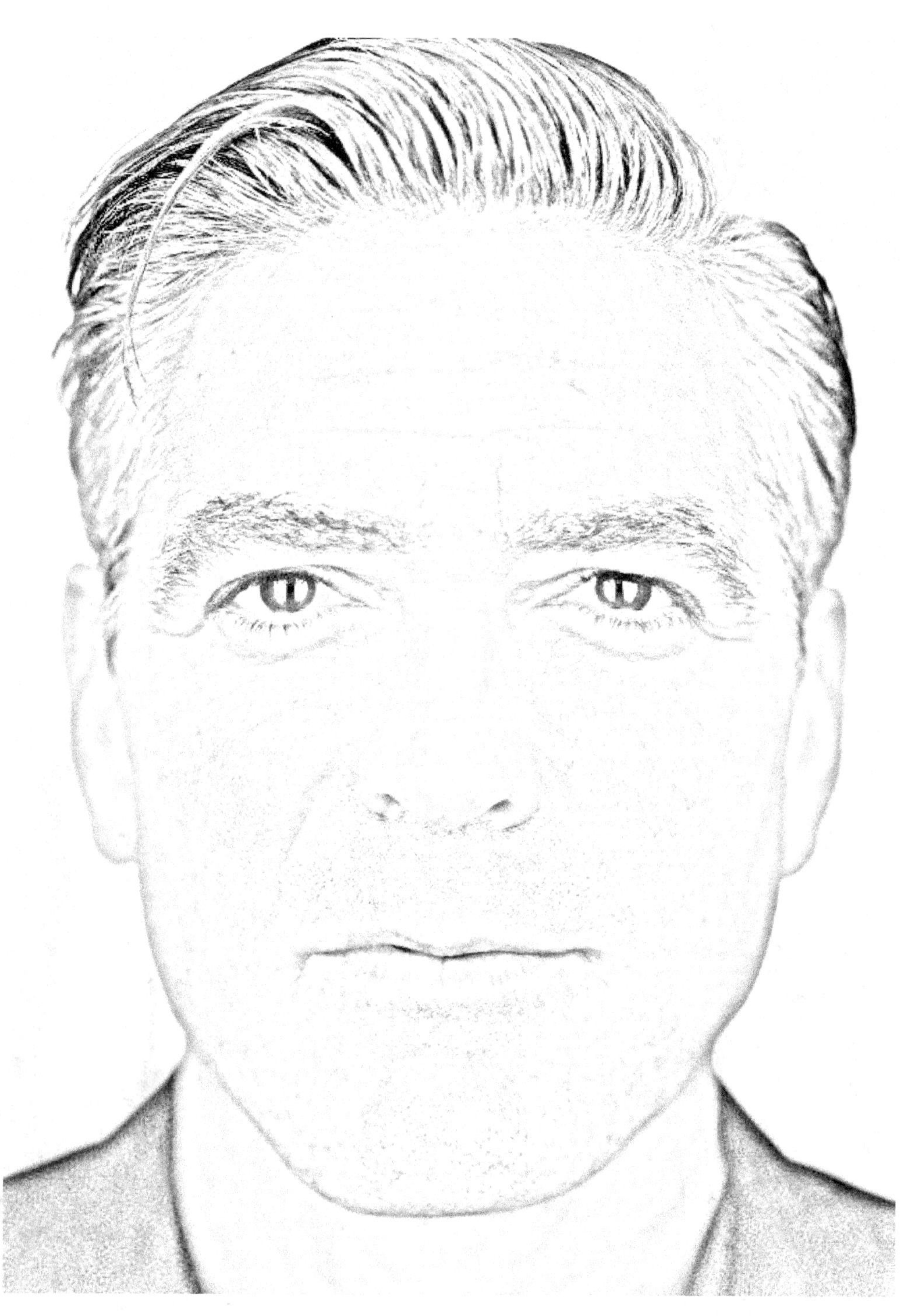

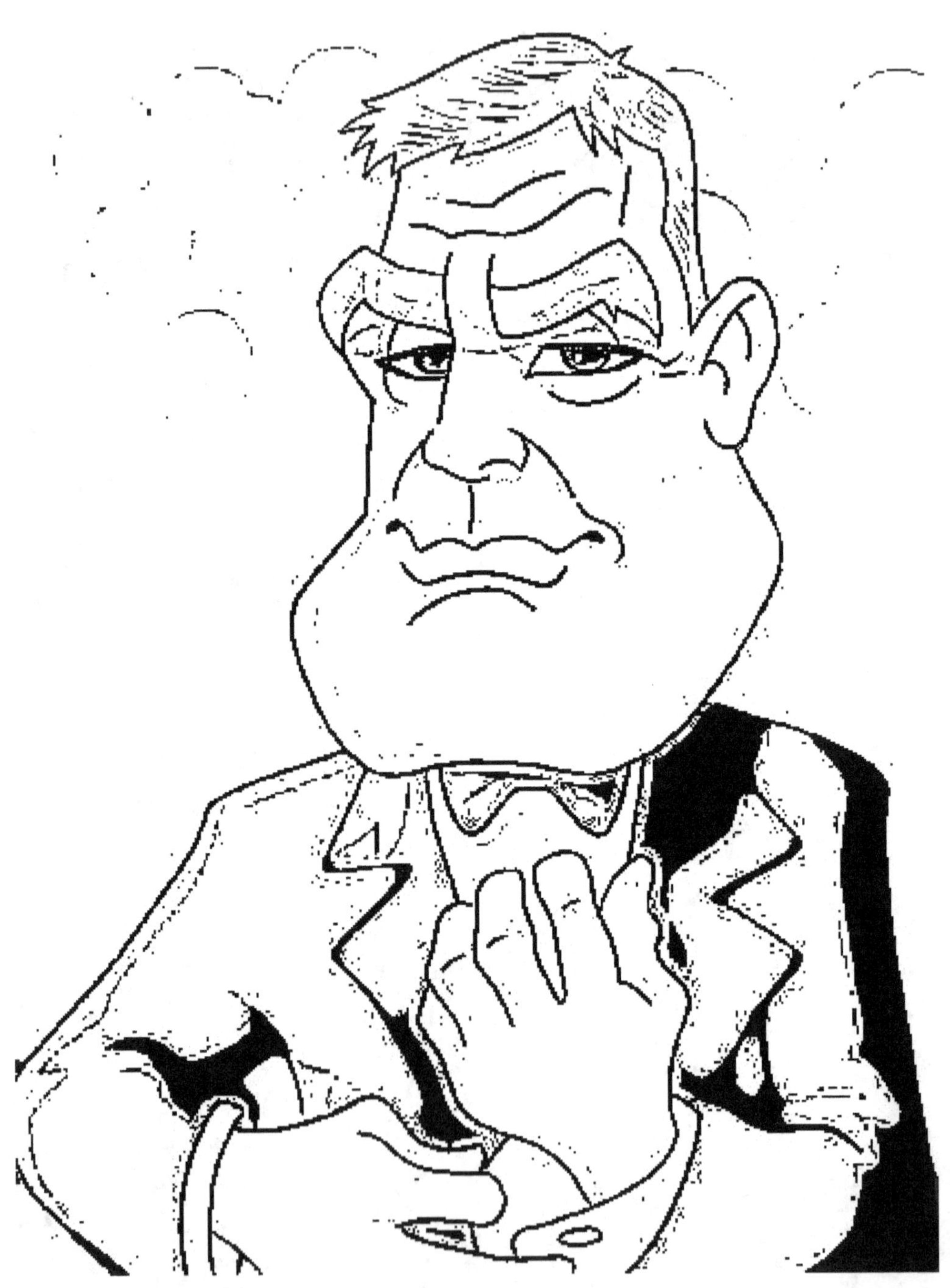

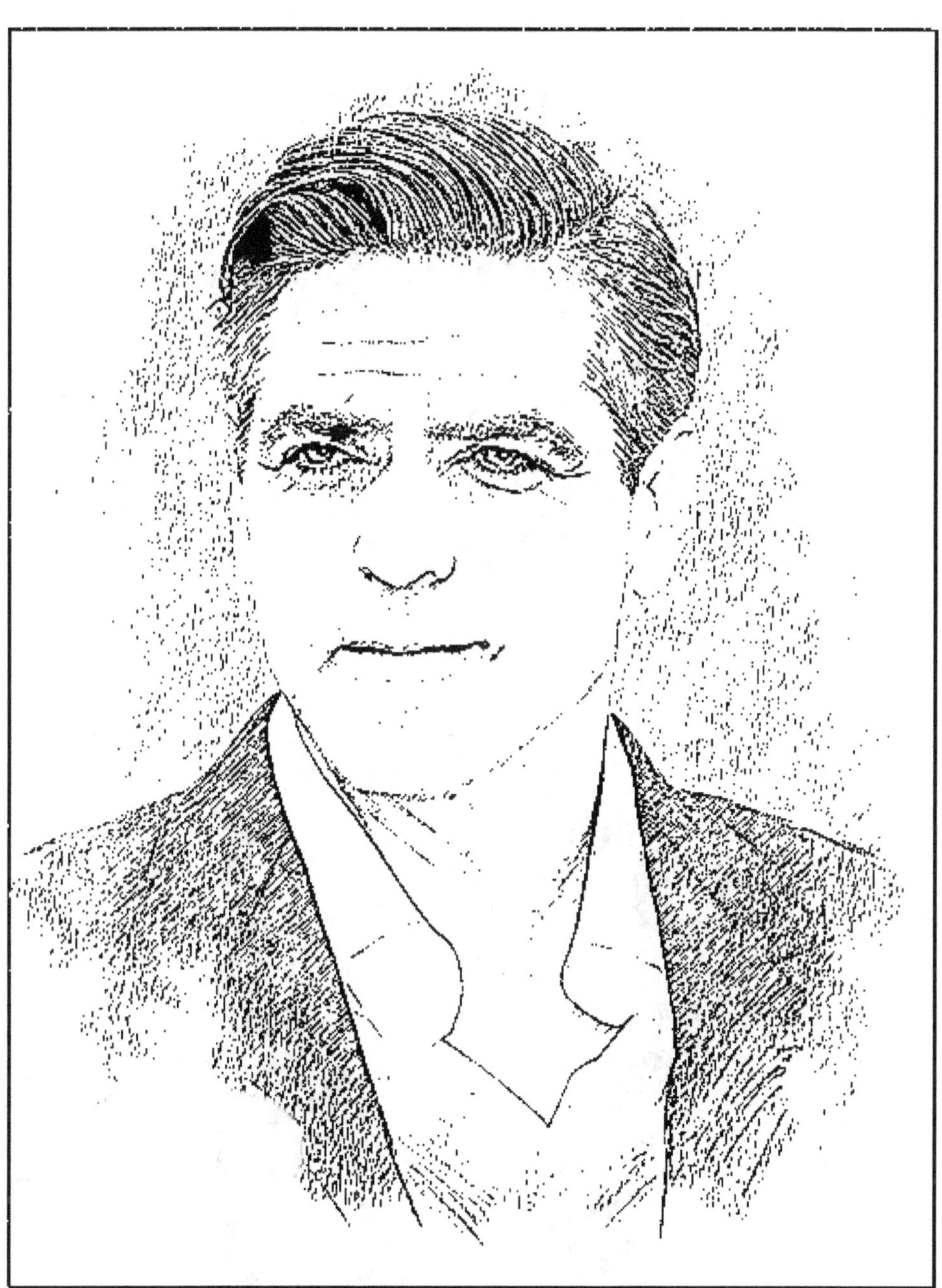

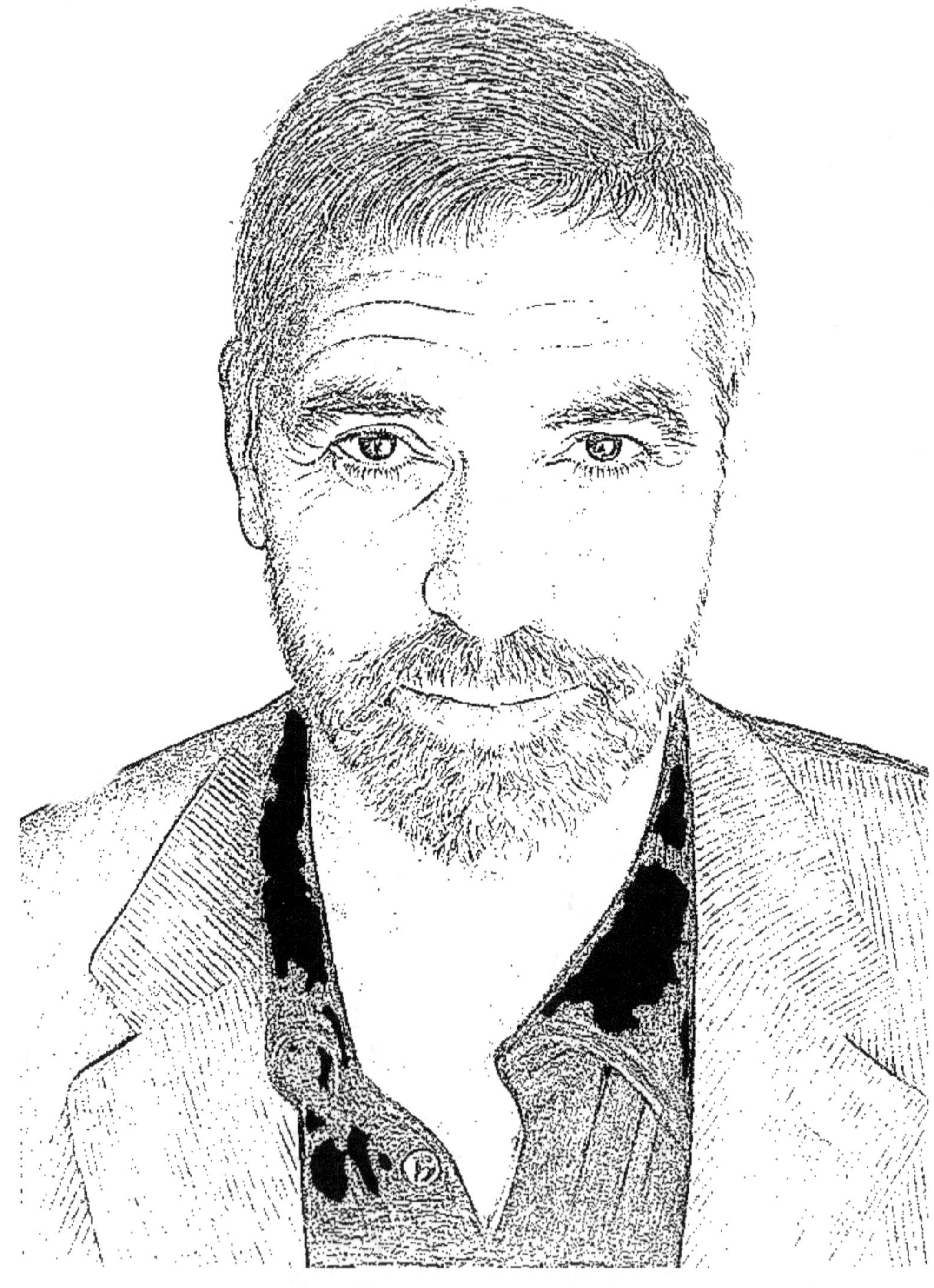

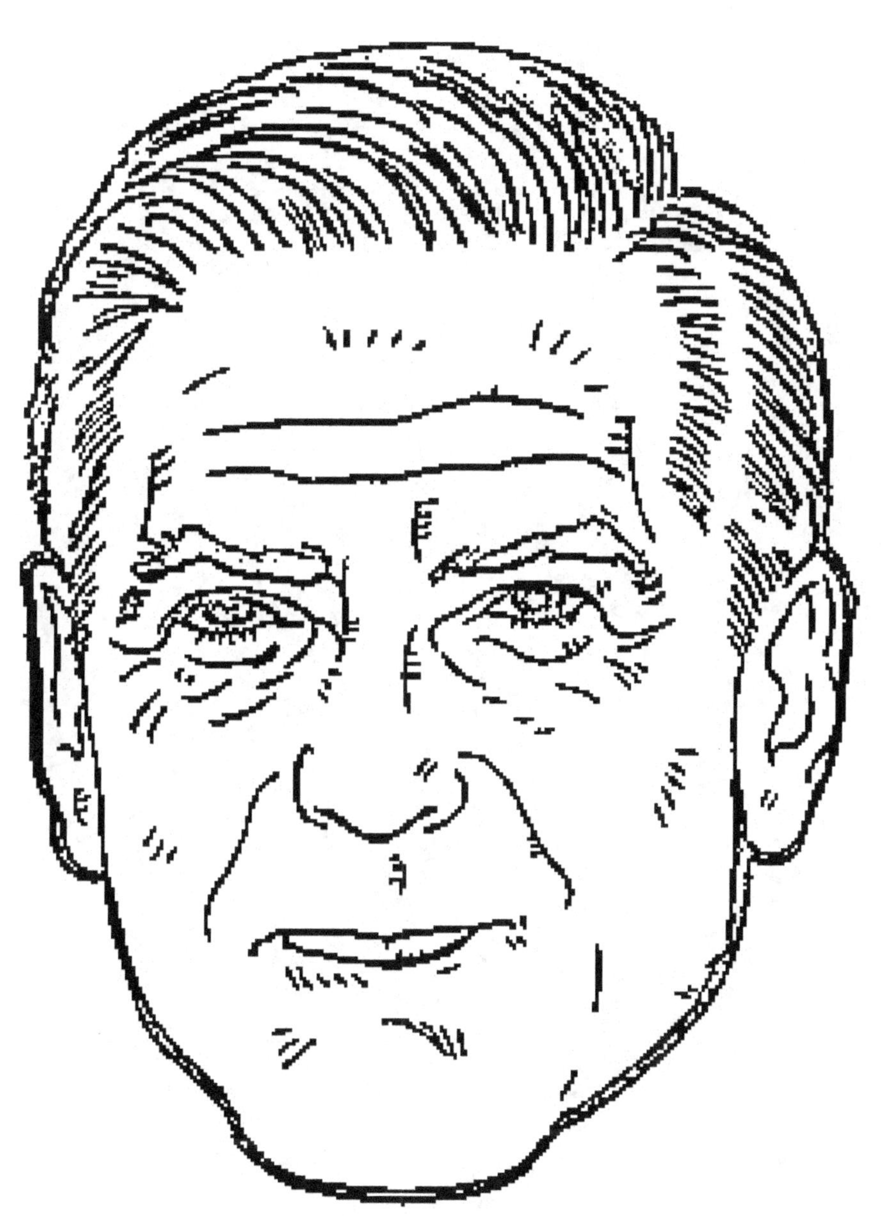

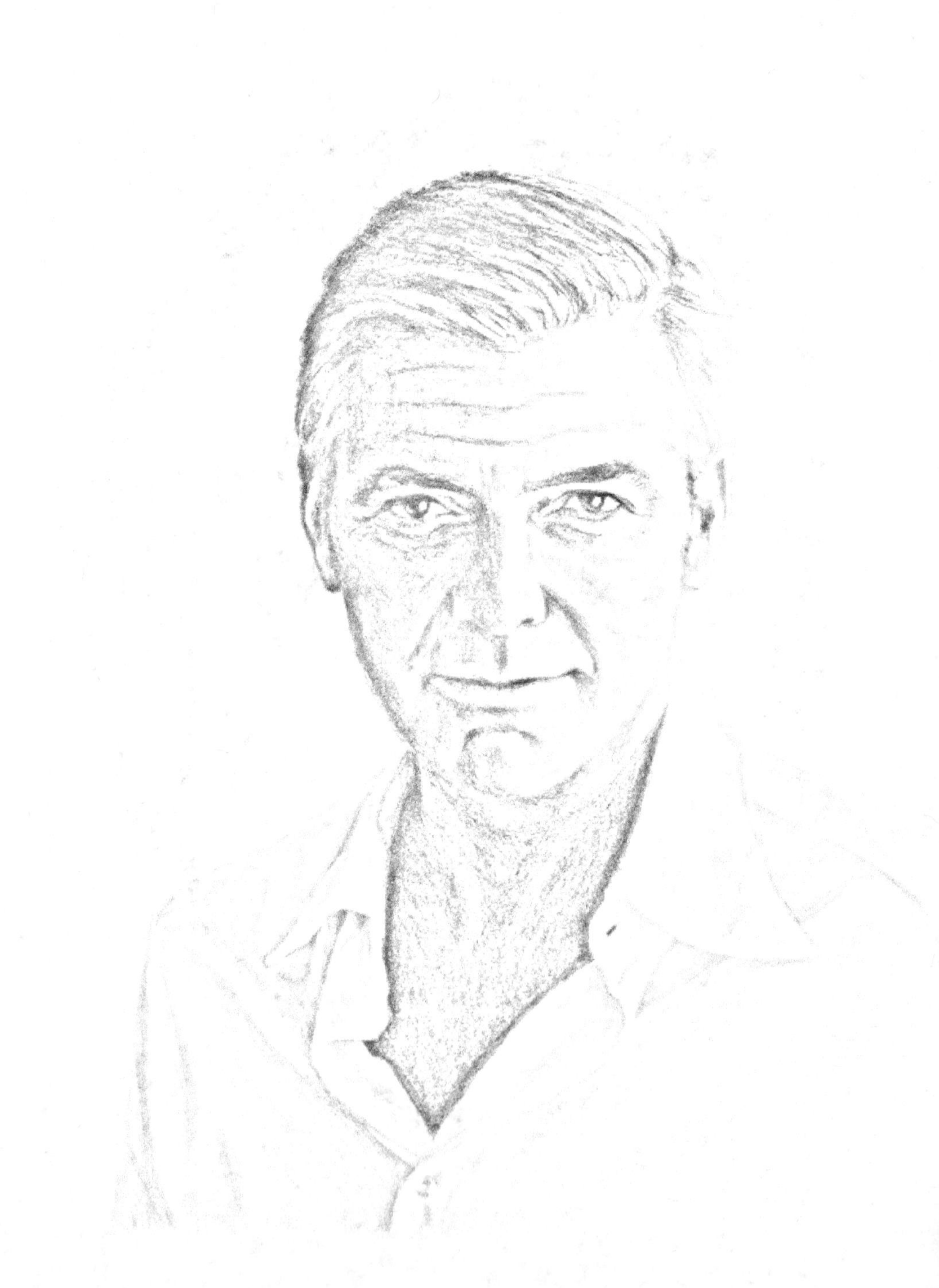

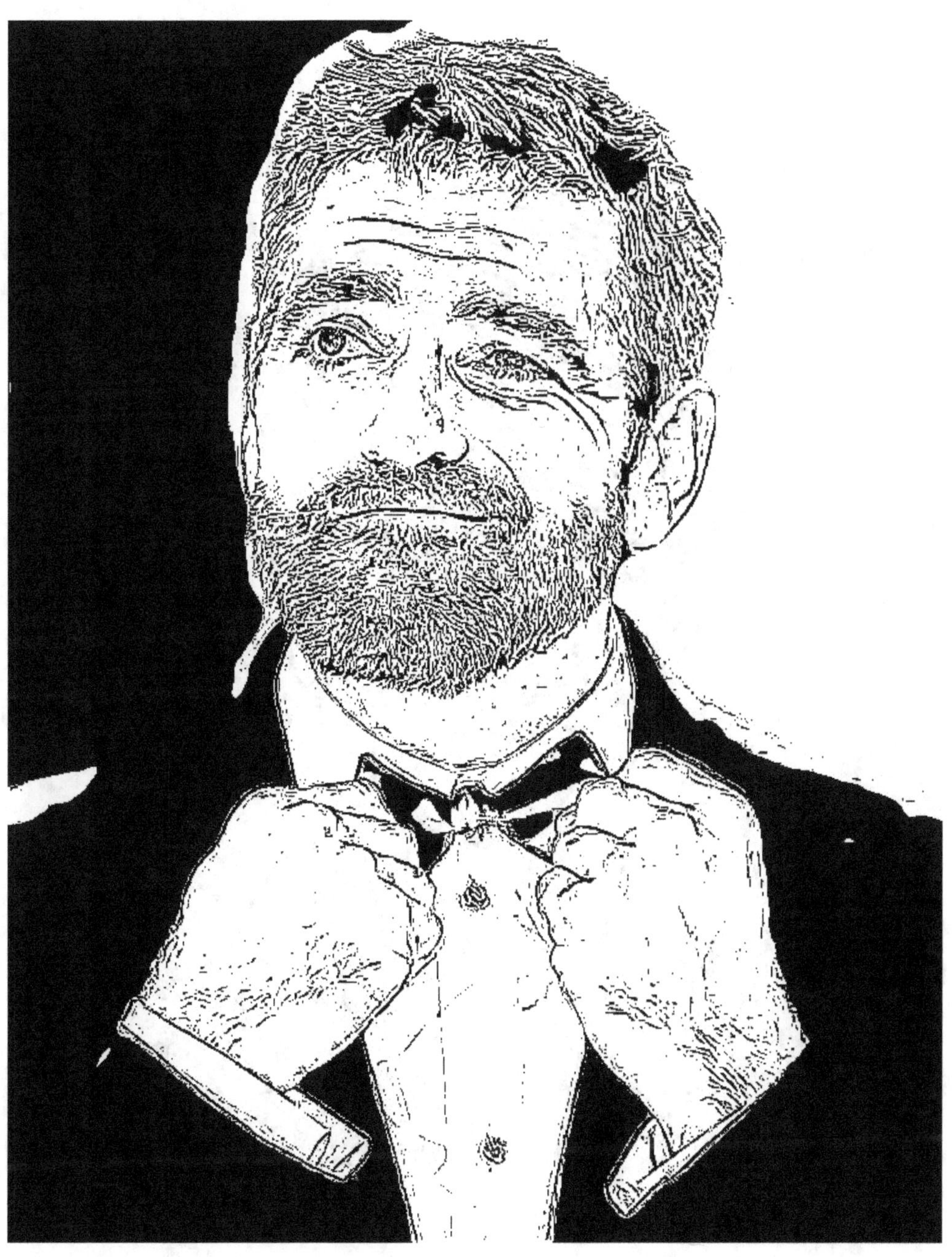

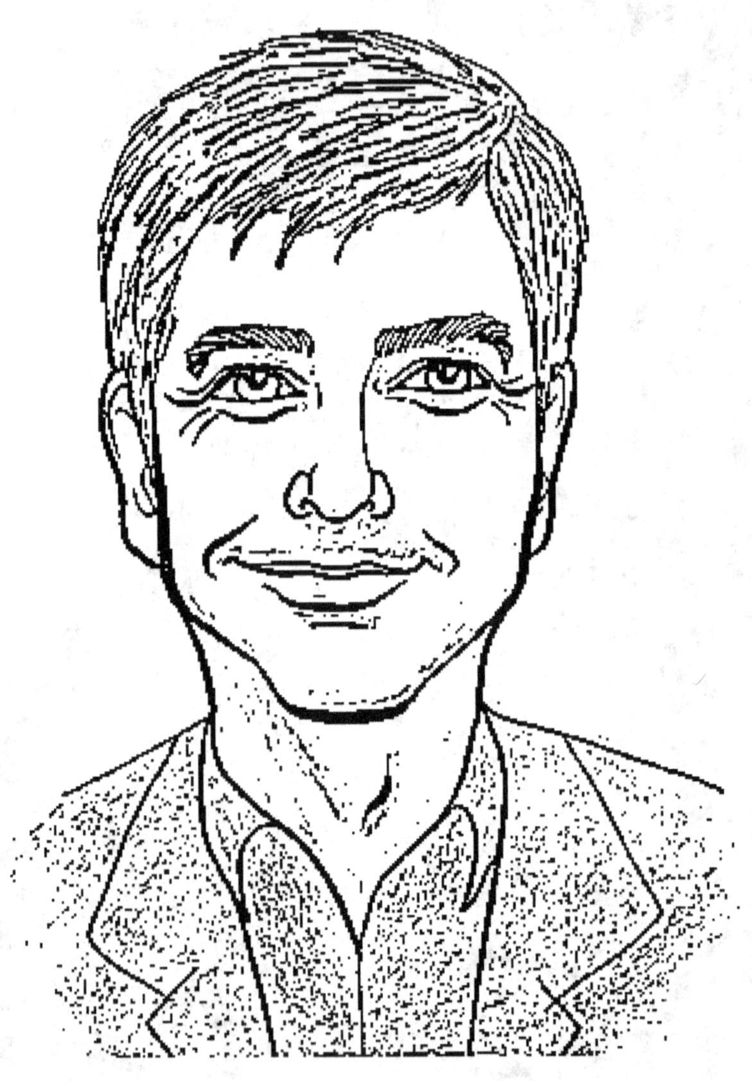

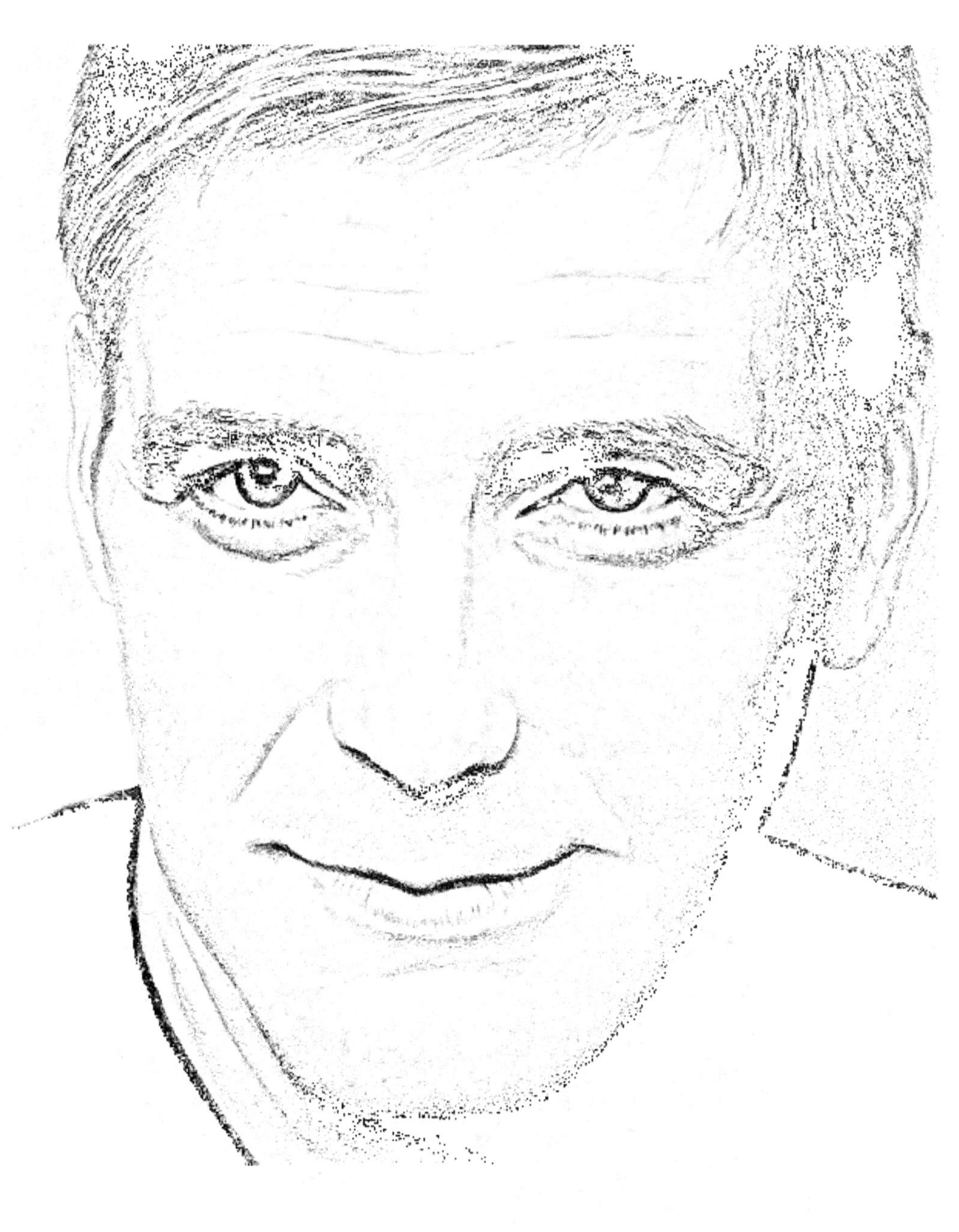

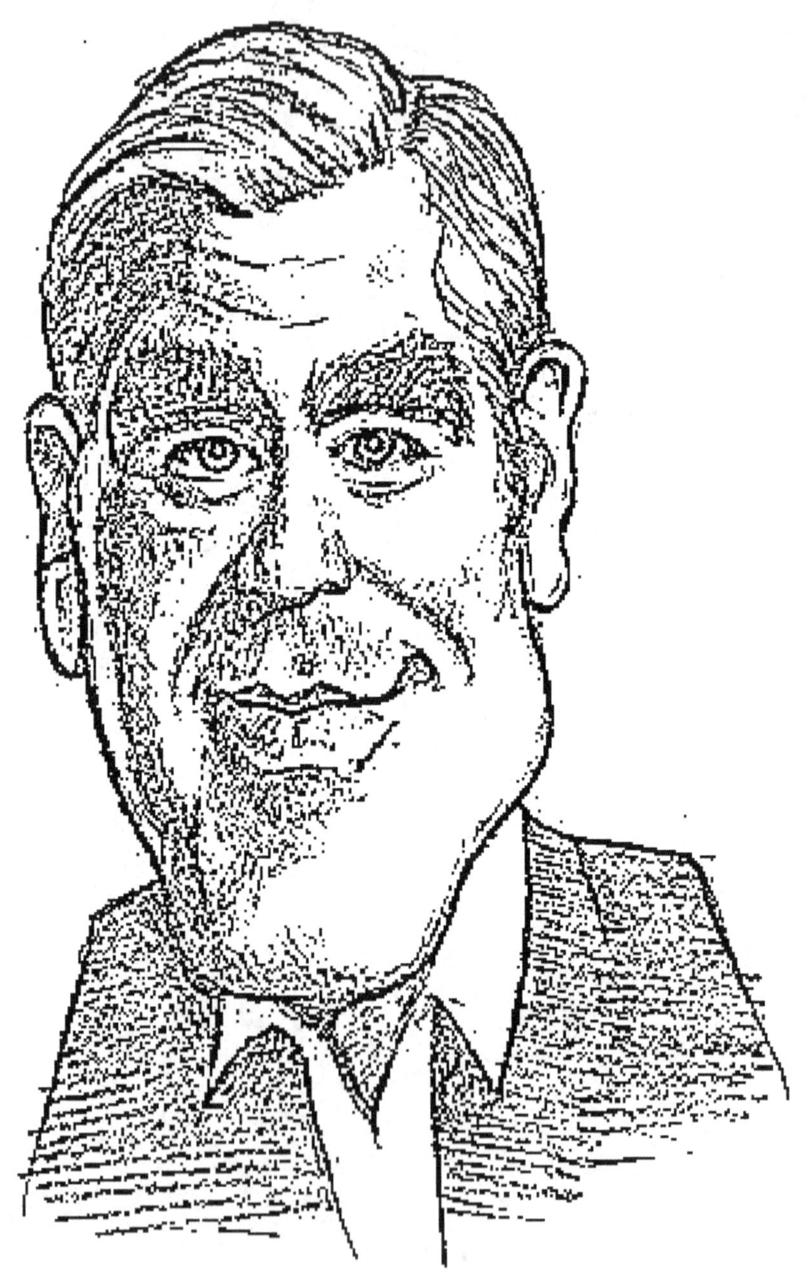

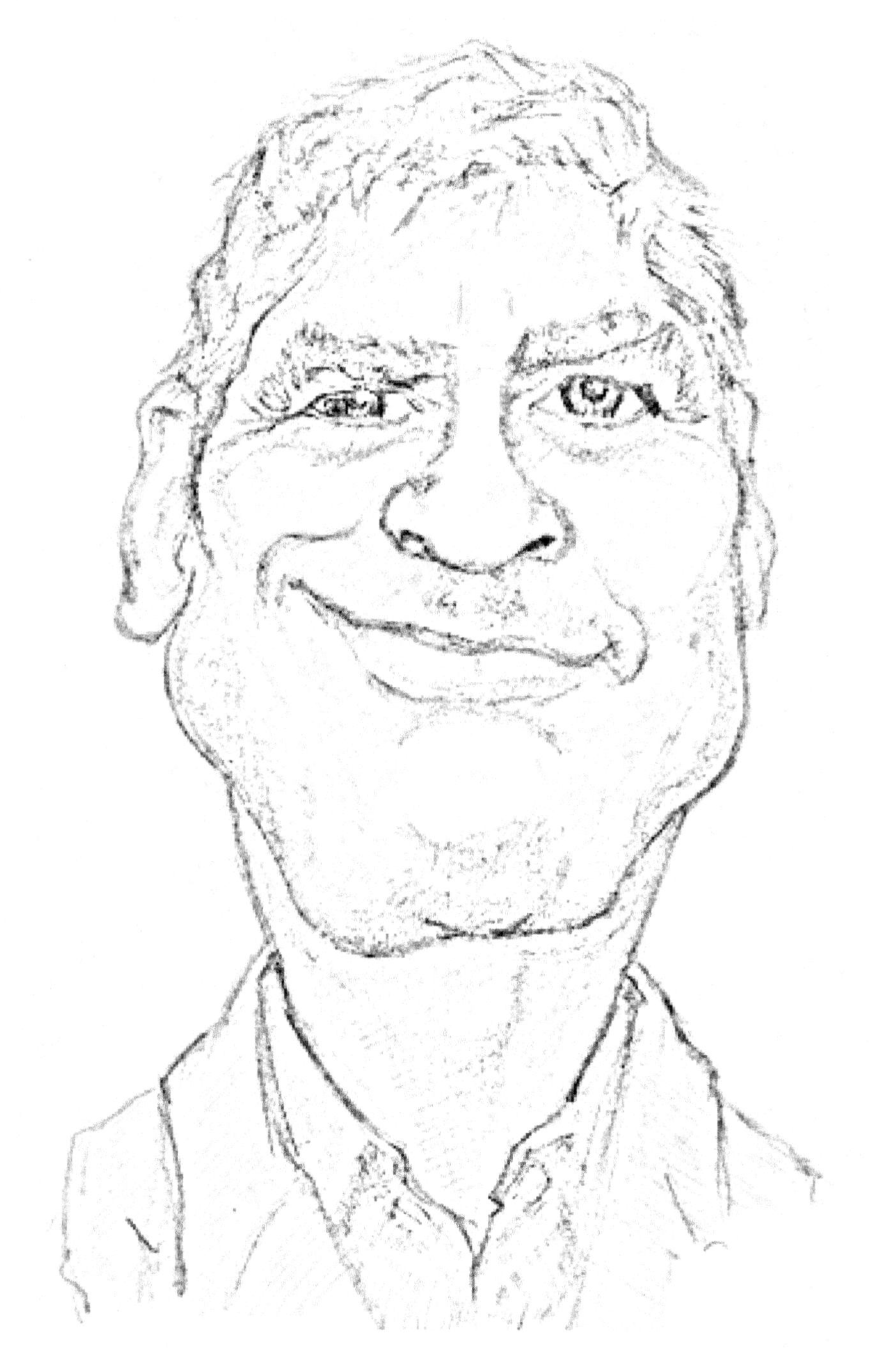

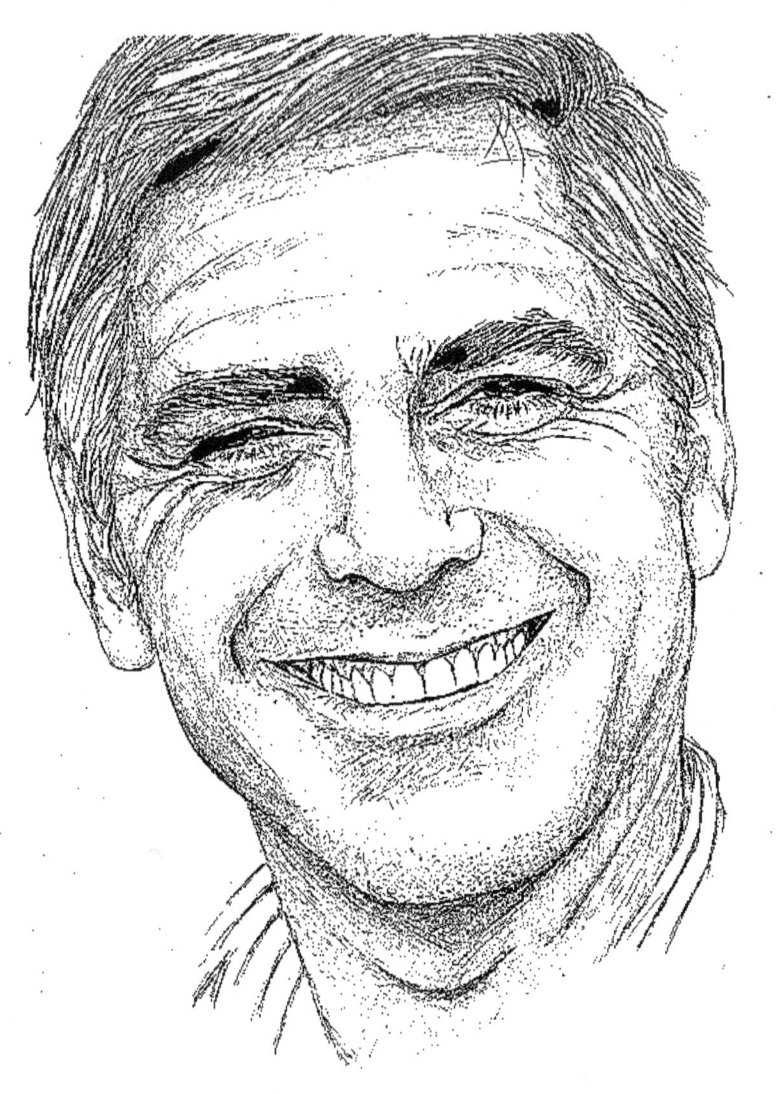

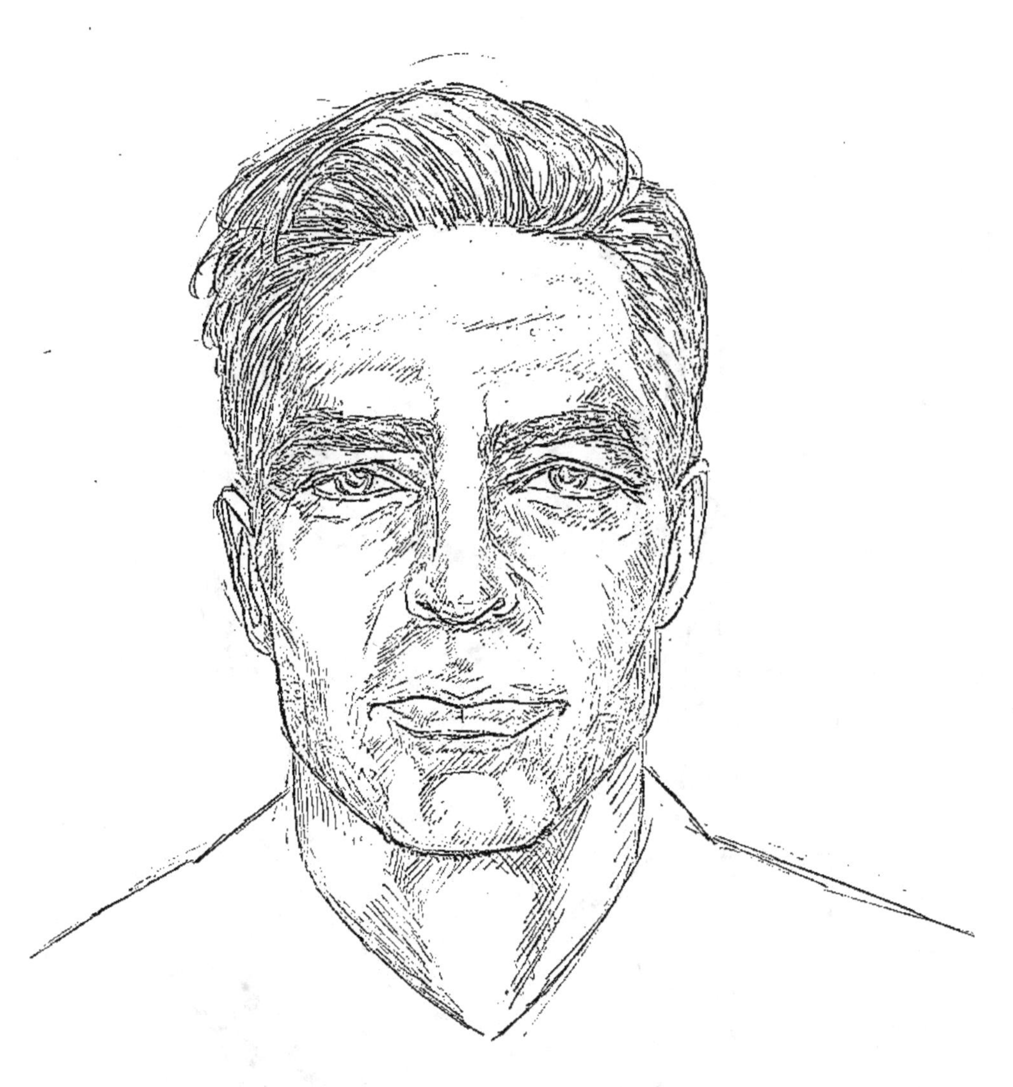

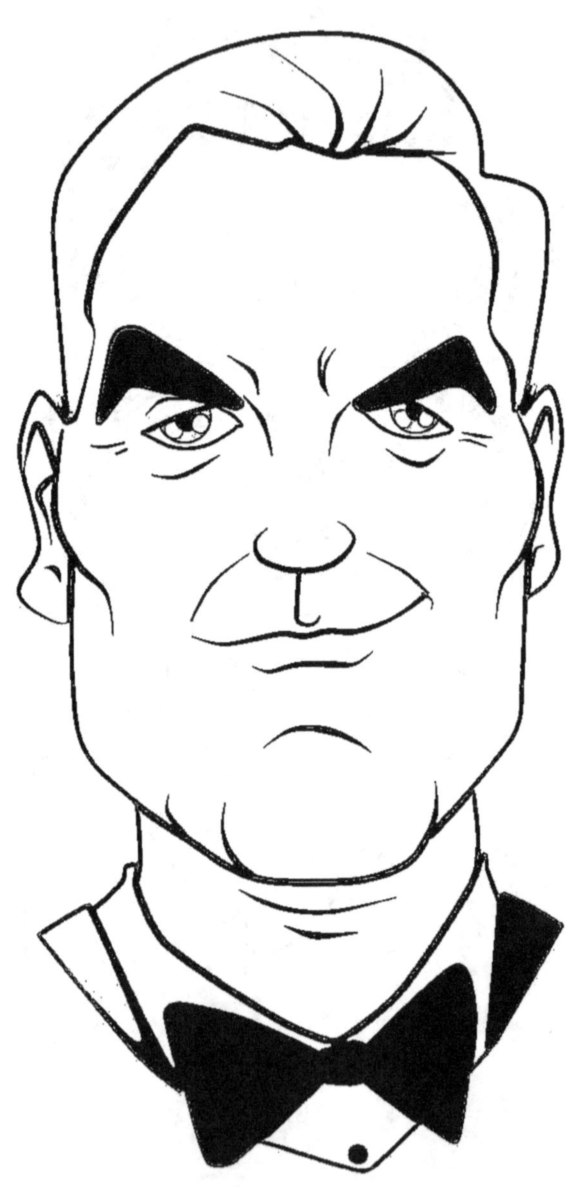

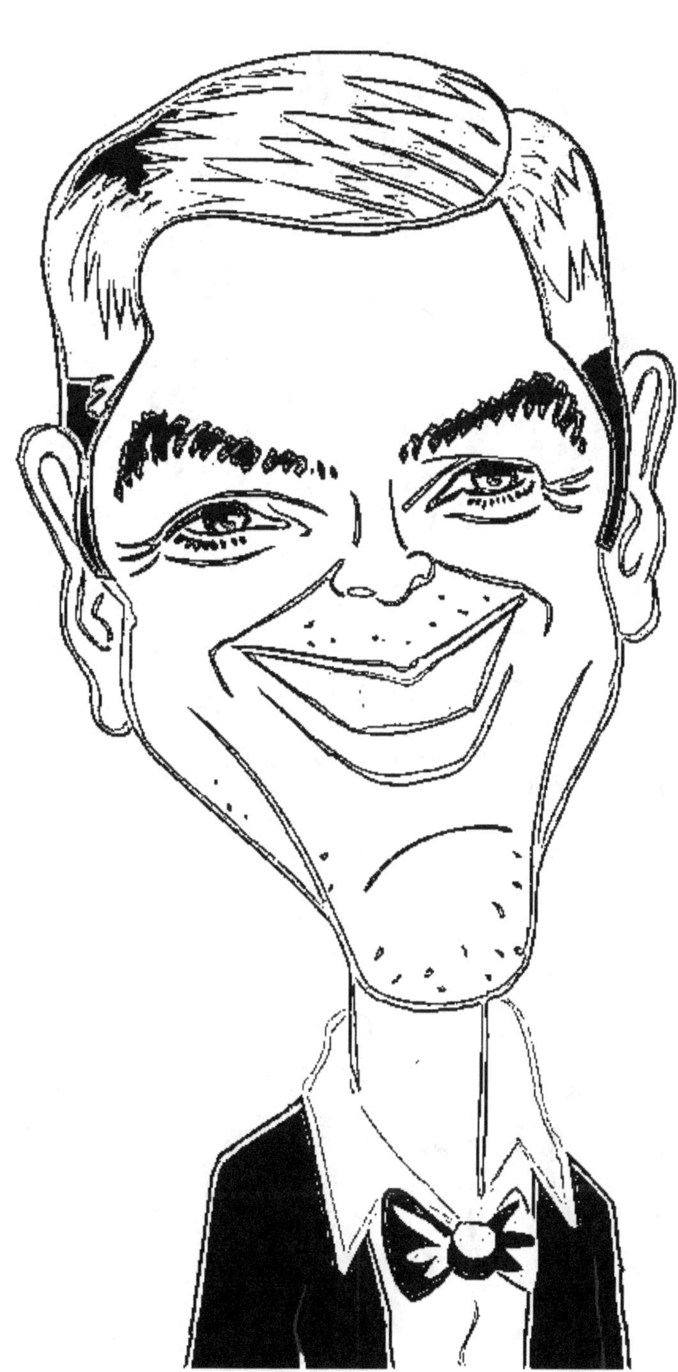

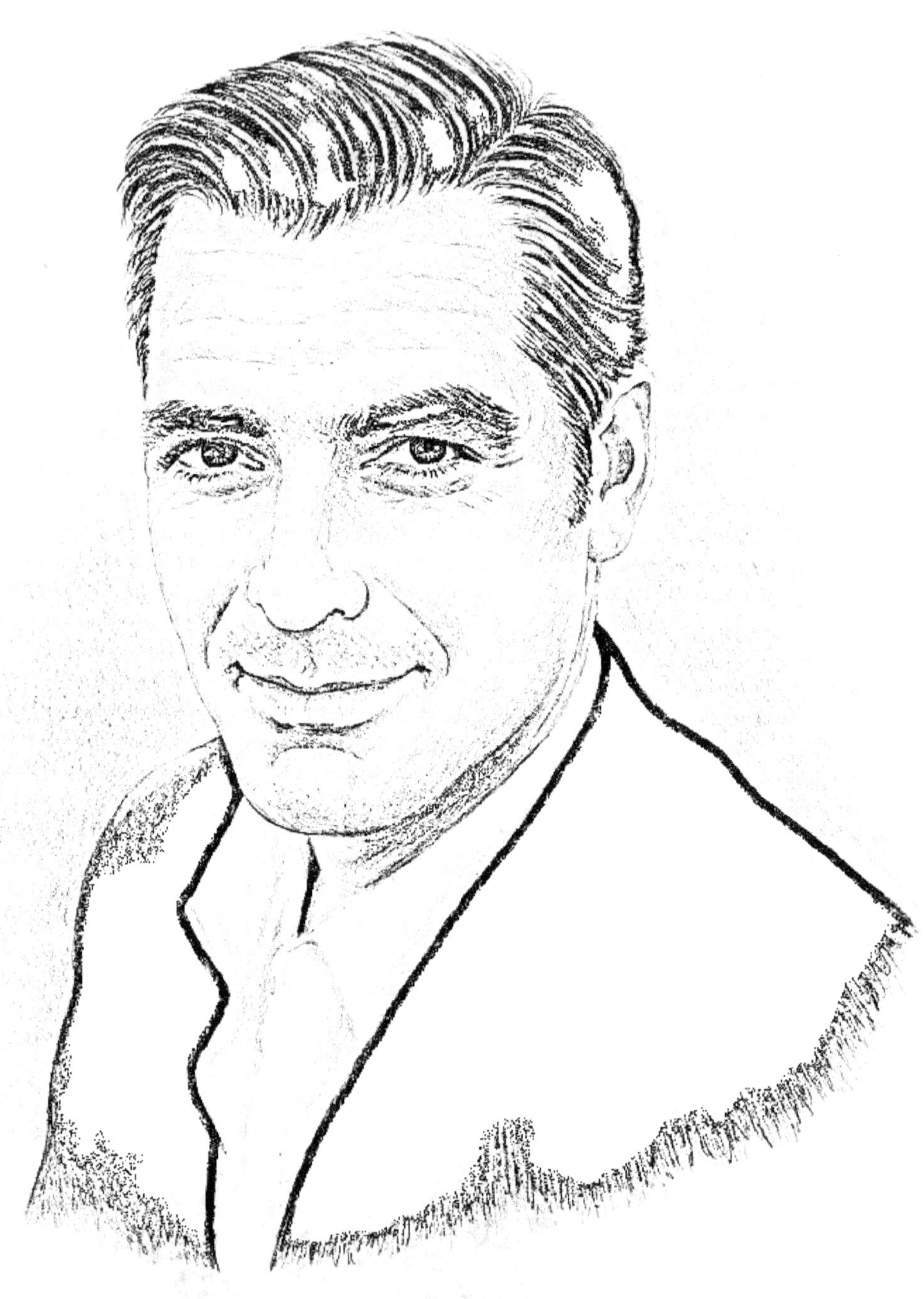

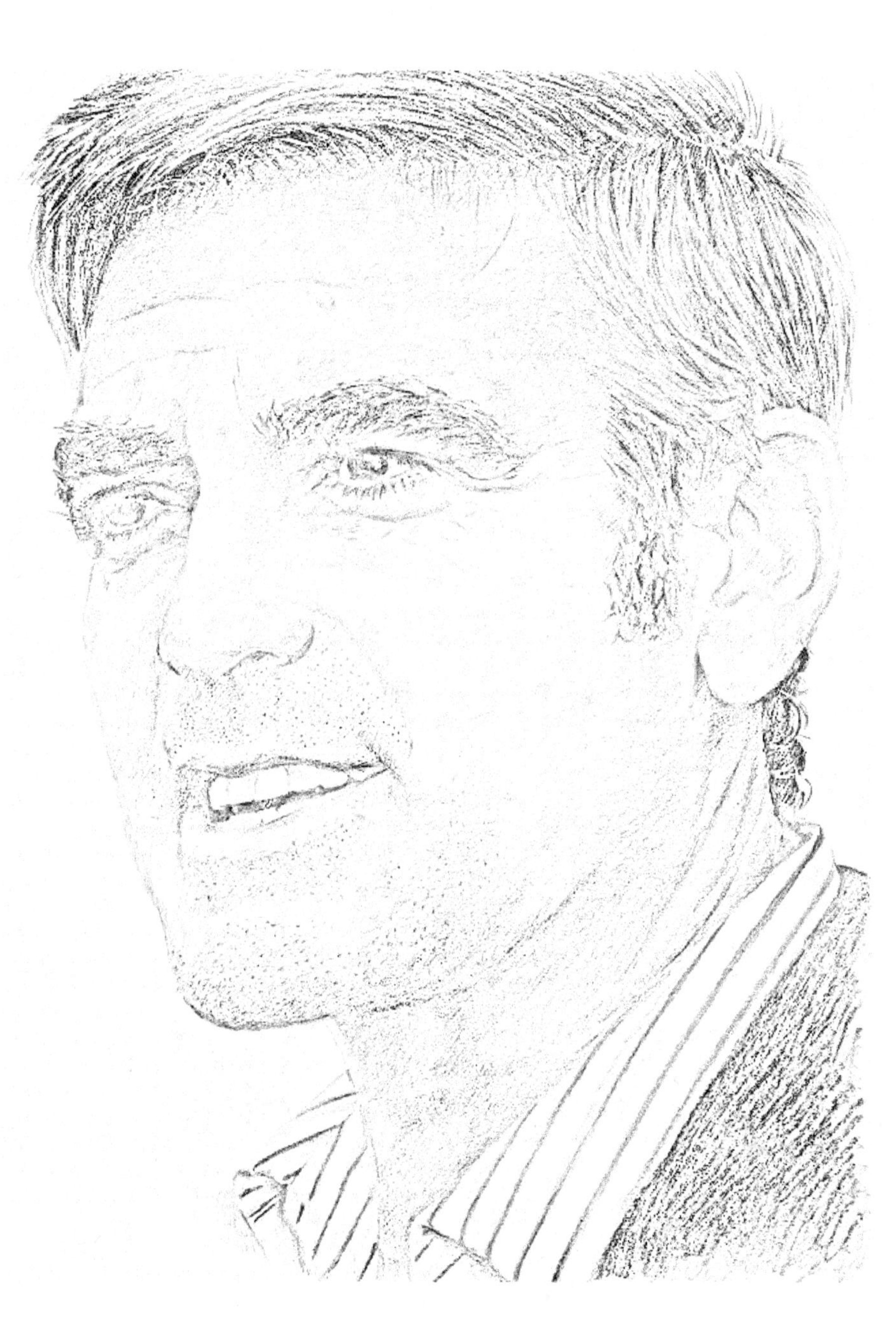

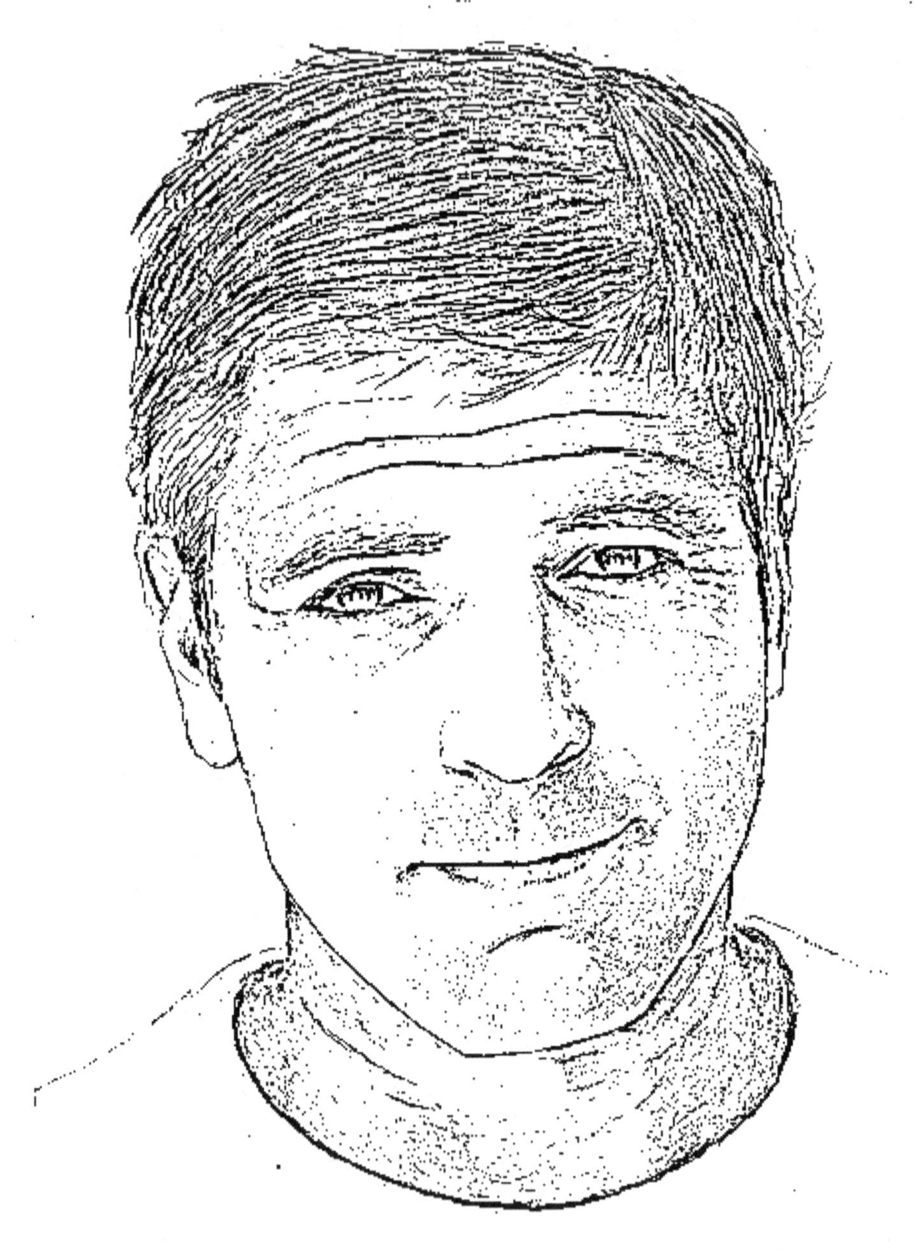

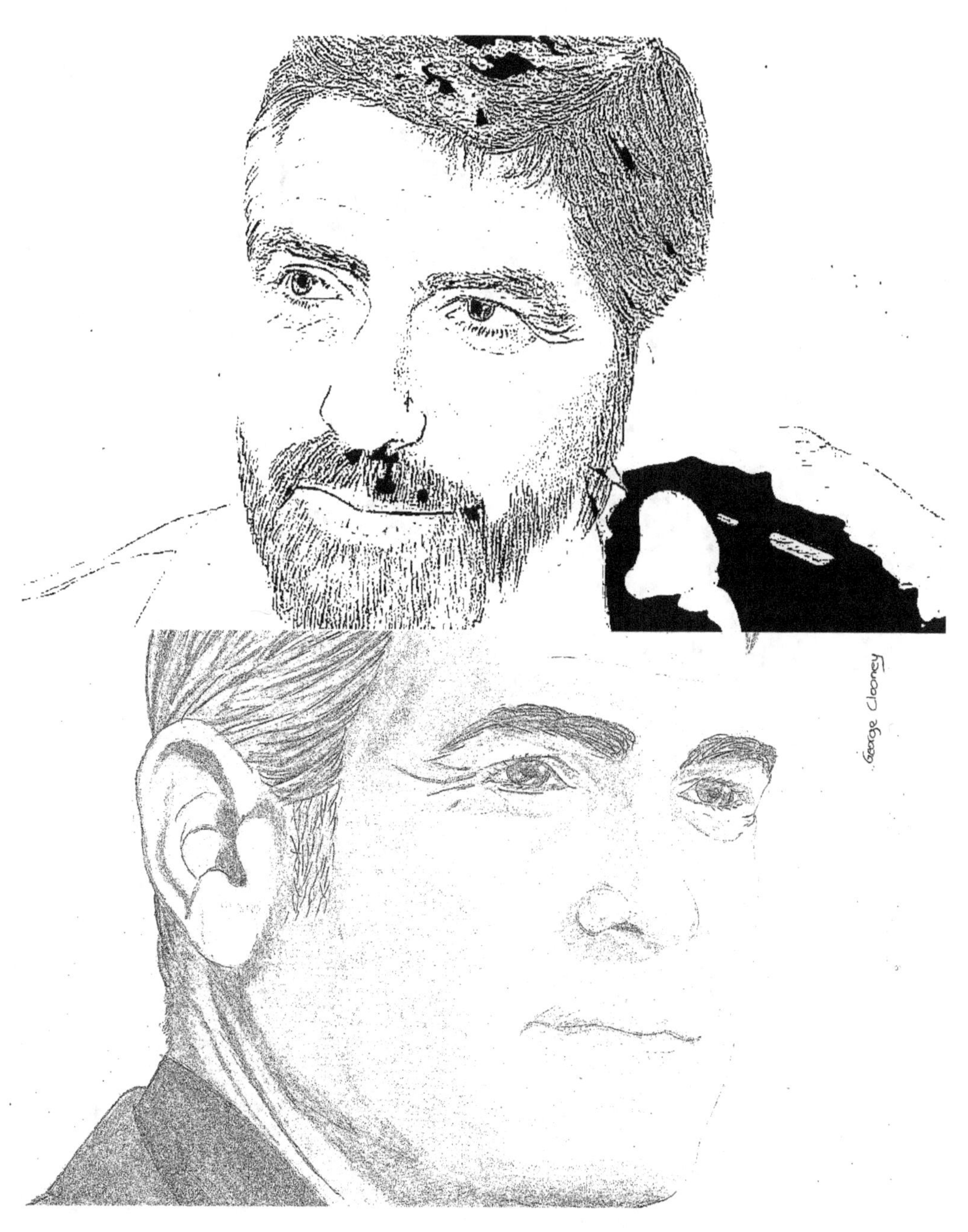
George Clooney

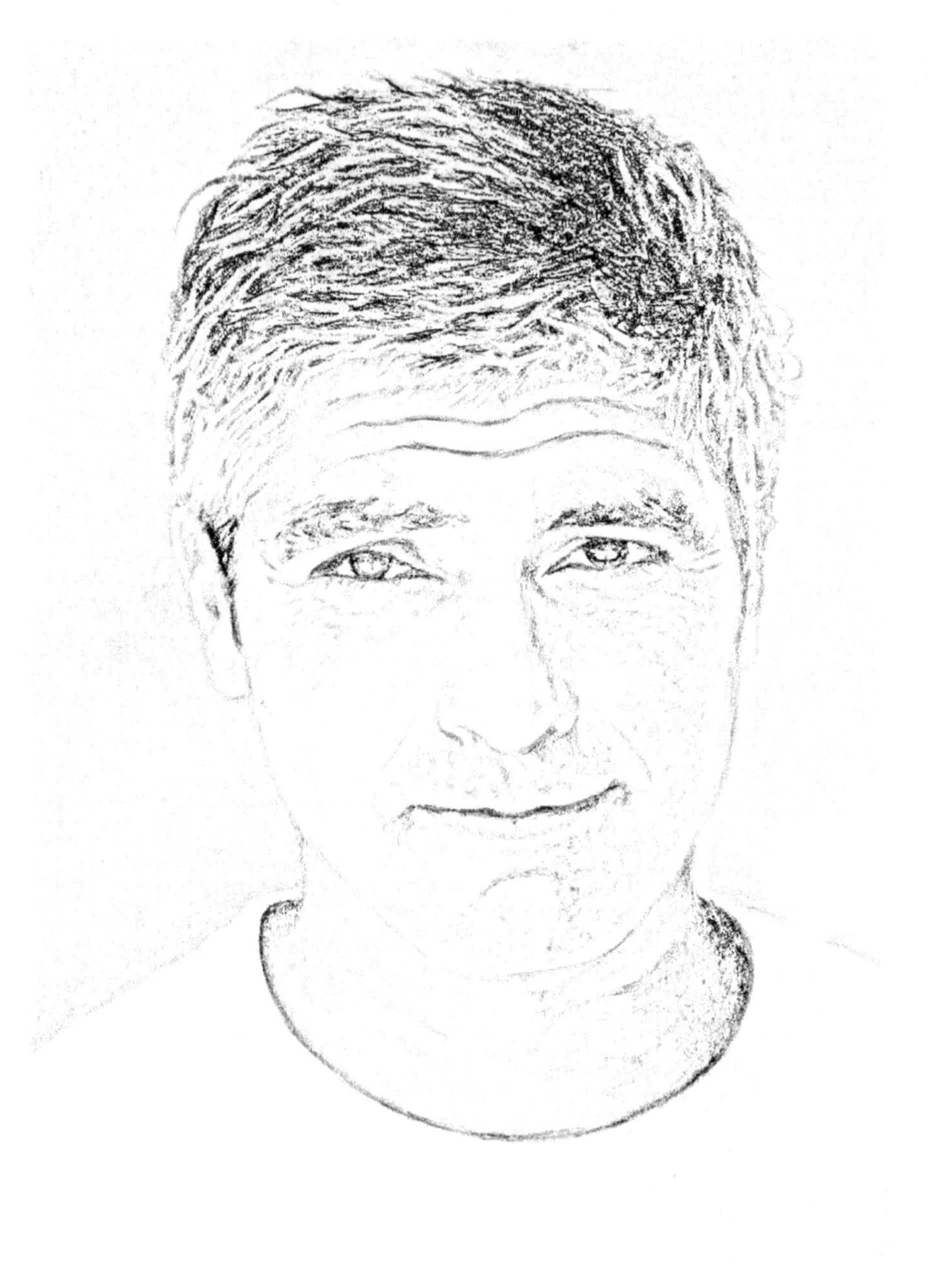

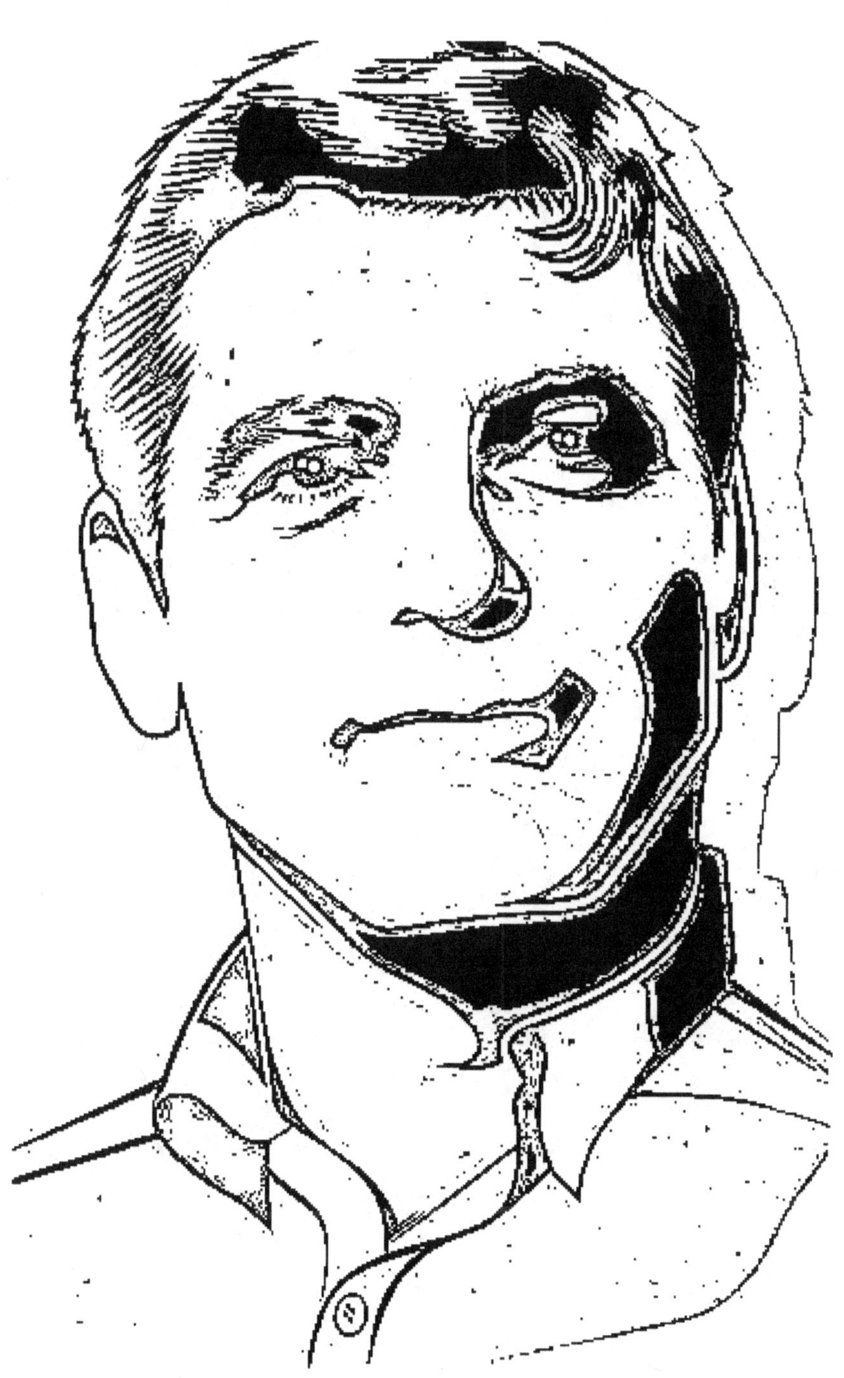

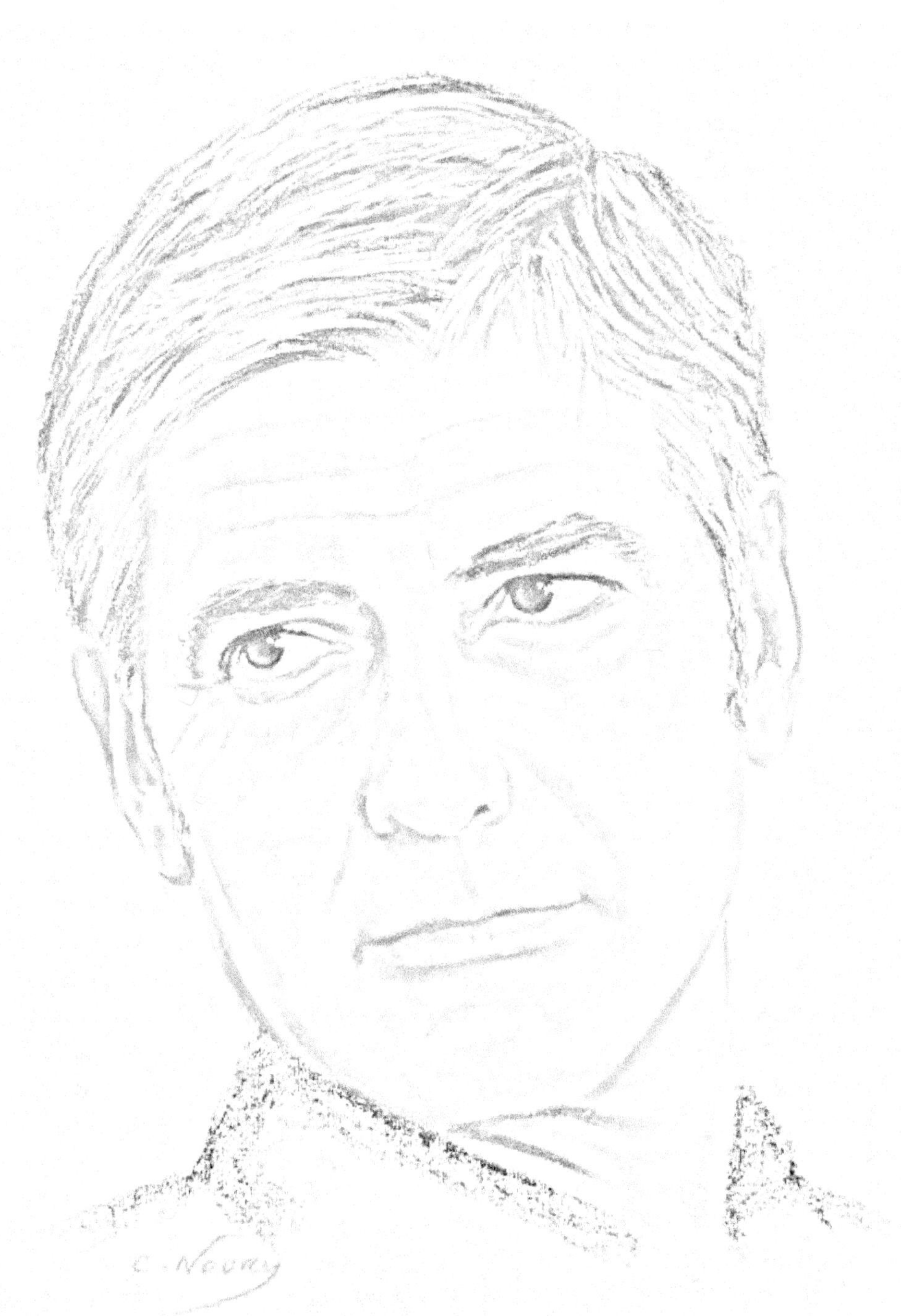

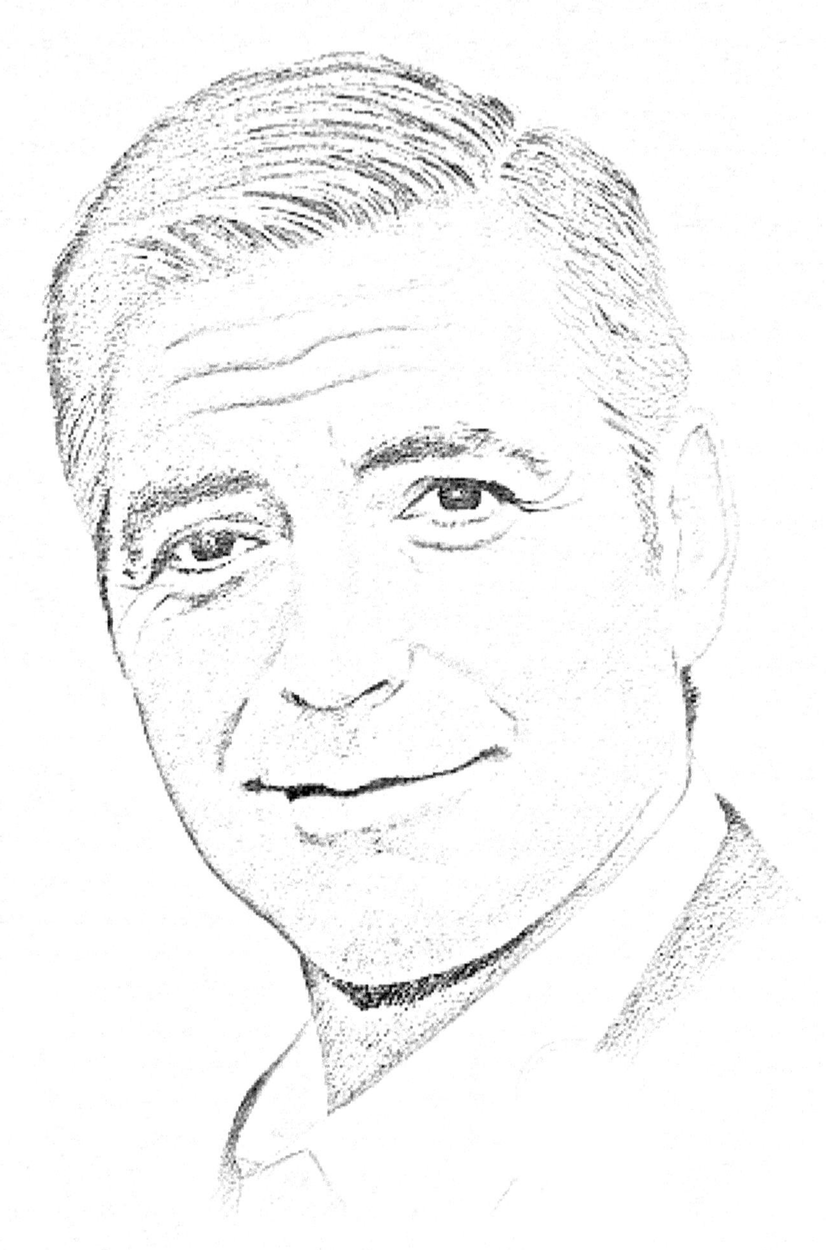

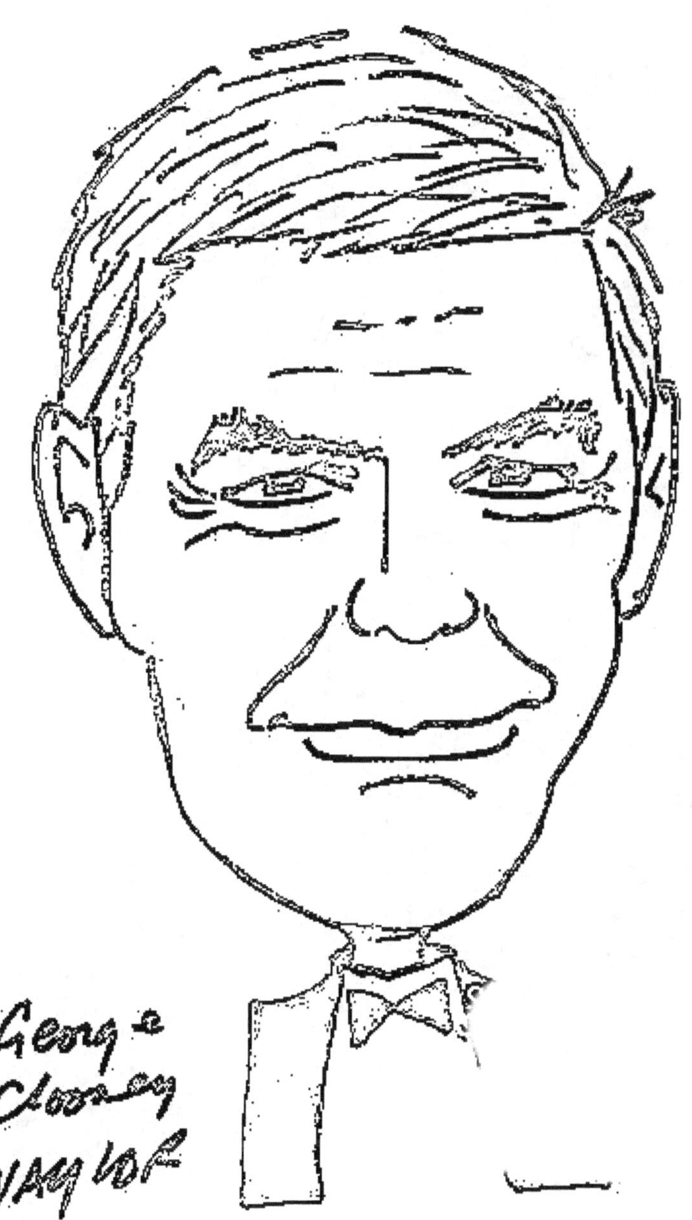
Georgie
Clooney
Naylor

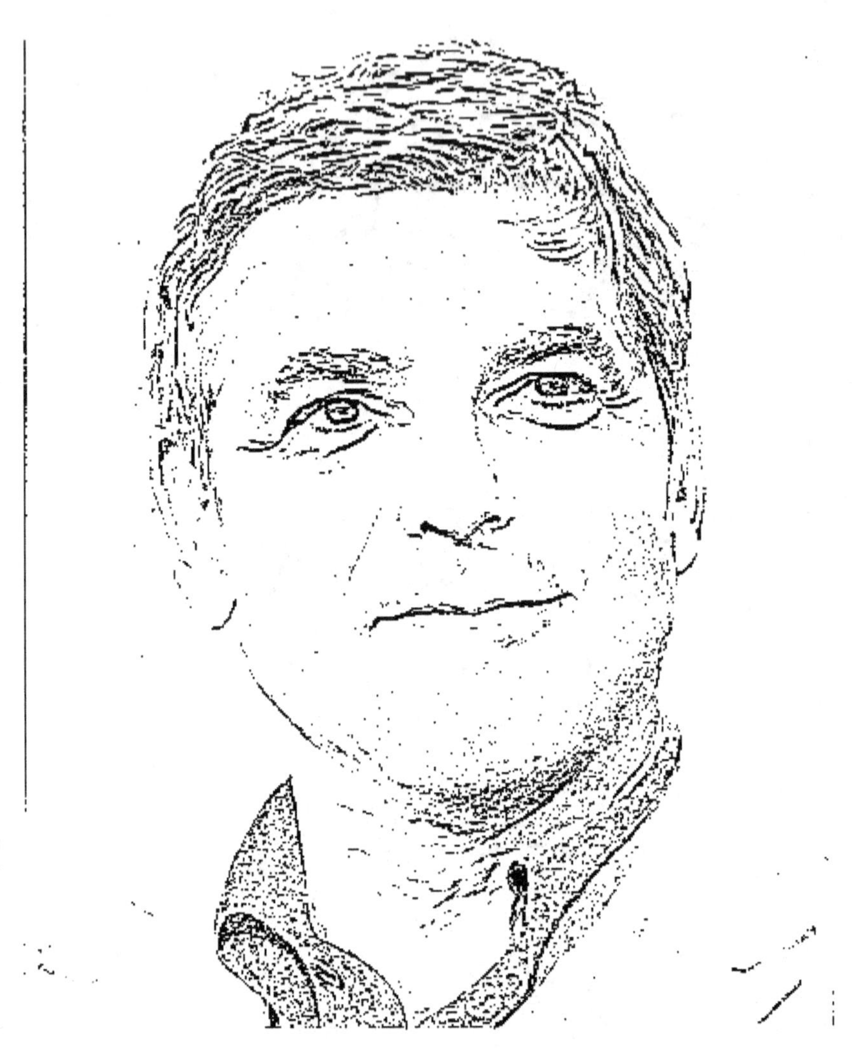

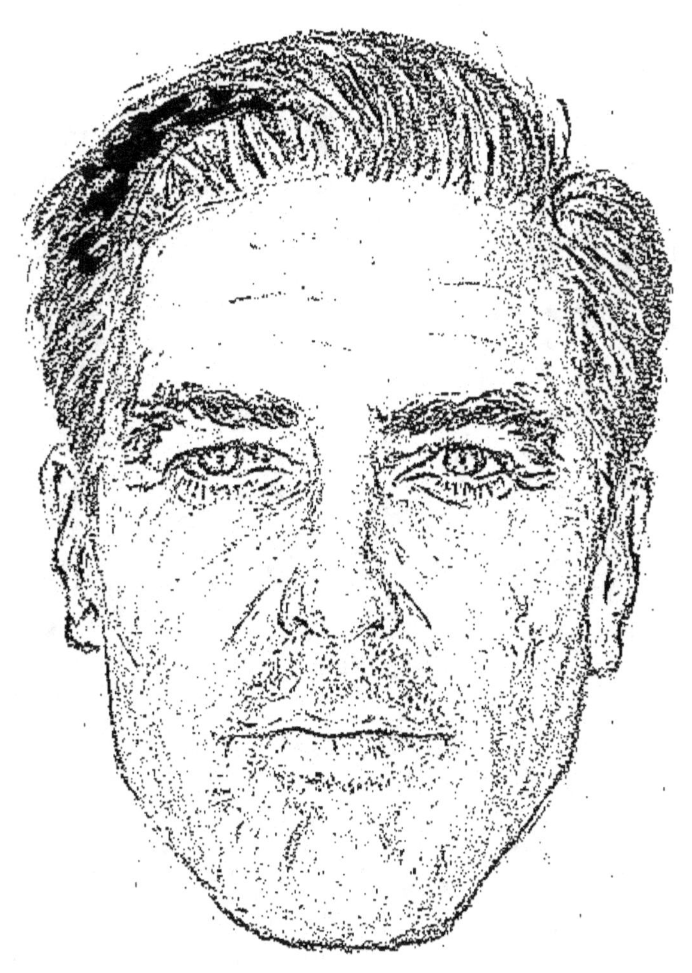

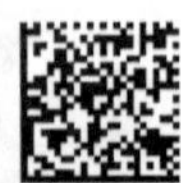